LAST DAYS ON THE NILE

Also by Malcolm Forsberg:

LAND BEYOND THE NILE

LAST DAYS
ON
THE NILE

Malcolm Forsberg

✖✖✖✖✖✖✖✖✖✖✖✖✖✖✖✖✖✖✖✖✖✖

J. B. LIPPINCOTT COMPANY
Philadelphia and New York

TO ENID

APPRECIATION

Our Sudan mission family has been broken up. Some of its members are widely scattered in their home countries, Australia, New Zealand, Britain, Canada, and the United States. Others have been absorbed into our larger fields where the work continues: Somali Republic, Ethiopia, Lebanon, Nigeria, Dahomey, and Liberia. This is their story.

Their loyalty to the Sudan persists. They conducted themselves honorably in that country. I have not had to apologize for any of them. I am indebted to them and to members of other missions for giving me information about their work and for checking what I had written.

College Church in Wheaton gave me the use of an office, which enabled me to get away from it all in the early hours of the morning. The First Presbyterian Churches in Tacoma, Washington and Flushing, New York, the Garfield Baptist Church in Milwaukee, and the Dieringer Bible Church near Tacoma continue to support us though our status has changed from overseas missionary to home staff member.

My own family endured with patience my preoccupation with writing and the dull thud of the typewriter.

Members and officers of the Sudan Interior Mission encouraged me and gave their blessing. We have spent all the years of our adult lives in the work of the S.I.M. We cherish our relationships in our Mission.

Julia Phillips Zimmerman did the last typing of the manuscript—a big job.

Muriel Fuller, my literary agent in New York, read the manuscript when it was less than half finished. She encouraged me to go ahead. Her direction and help and criticism and her arrangements for publication were major factors in bringing the writing of this book to a successful conclusion.

FOREWORD

This was not an easy book to write. We loved the Sudan, its deserts and its swamps, its plains and its bush country. We loved its people, Northerner and Southerner. During the last ten years we looked on as these people tried to solve some serious national and personal problems.

As missionaries we remained outside the active discussion of national affairs. But we had deep feelings of sympathy toward the Sudanese in their extremity.

After the country became independent, it was governed most of the time by a small minority, the Army. The minority did not always represent the concerns of the majority.

This book had to tell the story of the actions taken by the minority. Our love and respect for the Sudanese majority, North and South, remains. Our missionaries, though expelled from the country by the military authorities, harbor no resentments.

Our daily prayers offered during the last ten years tell the story: "Oh, Lord, help the Sudanese to find a way out of their difficulties that Northerners and Southerners may learn to respect each other and to live in peace." Such prayers were not formal. They came from the heart and they continue to be offered.

Missionaries would be happy to return to the land and people they learned to love. More important than their return is the need of the Sudanese themselves to find a way that will allow all citizens to enjoy freedom and security and to have their daily needs supplied.

When the Sudanese have these assurances together with the freedom to practice and to propagate their various faiths, they will be able to look ahead to a bright and prosperous future. May God help them to find the way.

CONTENTS

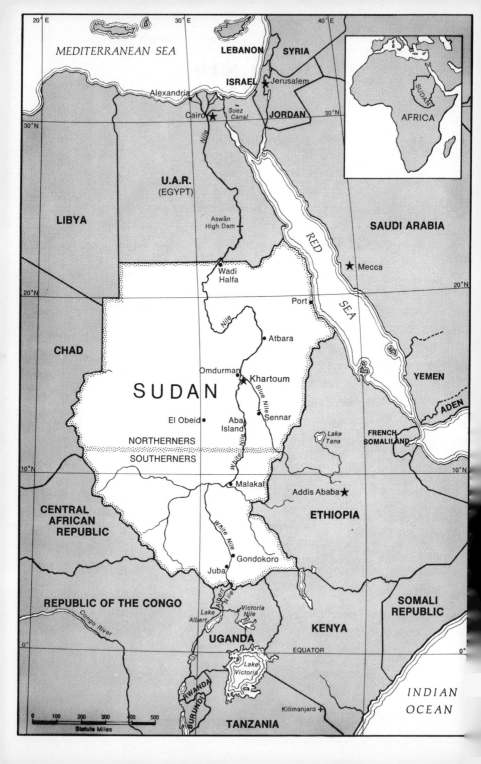

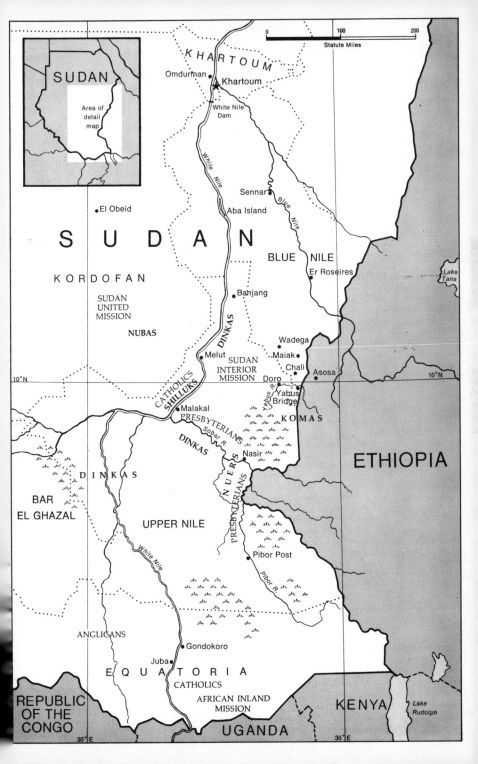

1

No Rebels

IT WAS MARCH 1964. The doctor bent over the baby. Sweat flowed down his face, his arms, his body. The sweat was induced by a devilish combination of temperature and humidity and by the tension surgery brings. He was removing a large tumor from the baby's face.

The two nurses wiped the perspiration from their hands as they passed instruments, dressings, sutures. Suddenly all was still. The door had opened and a tall form had entered the operating room. "This is it," the voice said. "The police have come to tell us we have seven days in which to pack up and leave."

The missionary who had entered the room to bring the news withdrew. He had work to do.

The operation was completed. Skin was grafted over the wound. Dressings were applied. The baby was removed to the ward. No more missionary surgery would be performed in the McQuilkin Memorial Hospital of the Sudan Interior Mission.

Doro, a village in the Republic of the Sudan, was no
African paradise. It was one of many villages of the
Nilotic Maban tribe which stretch westward from near
the Ethiopian border until they meet the villages of the
tall Dinka people near the White Nile. Doro was hot,
windy, dusty. Any missionary working there had to be
a dedicated person. Lindsay McClenny, the Sudan Interior Mission doctor at Doro, was a dedicated man.

Seven days would not be long enough for him to
sort and pack his personal and medical goods. More
important than his goods were the people who, in seven
days, would be without medical care. The doctor continued to make his rounds in the wards. He looked at
his two TB patients. They were making good progress
on the medication he was giving. Three men were recover-
ing from kala azar (pronounced kalazar) dread disease
of the Sudan. With the ending of their treatment, there
would be no hope. Most of the other patients would
recover. The government had ordered the expulsion of
the missionaries but it had made little provision for the
care of medical patients.

The packing went on night and day. Most of it was
done at night for during the day the missionaries were
surrounded by questioning tribespeople. Little could
be said about the reasons for the expulsion order. To
the end the missionaries were faithful to their convic-
tions. They would not alienate the people from their
government. What the authorities had done to alienate
their own people was another matter.

Dr. McClenny tried to soften the keen disappointment
of the eighty lepers under his care. The doctor and his

fellow missionaries had brought the first ray of hope these decaying people had ever known. The departure of the missionaries would mean a return of the slow, relentless destruction of their bodies. The new sulfone drugs in the hands of the doctor had meant that they could hope for an arresting of the disease; they could live; they could return to their own villages from which they had been outcasts. These hopes had been brutally crushed. They would return to their villages to die.

Dr. Lindsay McClenny and his fellow missionaries at Doro were not unprepared for the expulsion order. On February 12 the station radios had brought news from Missionary Aviation Fellowship, control for the radio hookup, "All transmitters must be dismantled." For nine years the missionaries had been linked to each other and to the outside world by radio telephone. Now they had to dismantle their sets. "The rebels might seize them and use them." In the Sudan Interior Mission area there were no rebels.

In a few days the next peremptory command came from the police, "Missionaries must not leave their stations until further notice!"

It was the evening report from the British Broadcasting Corporation that finally broke the news. "Three hundred missionaries have been ordered to leave the Southern Sudan by the Military Government." That was on February 27, 1964.

Then came March 3, the day of the baby with the tumor, the day of the sweat, the surgery, and the incredible words, "Seven days to pack and leave."

In Khartoum the Minister of the Interior in the Military Government had made his explanation of the expulsion order to the Central Council on March 4. "It is a source of profound satisfaction," he had said. Missionaries, he explained, had been generously treated. They had violated the hospitality of the Sudan. The government had been patient.

British imperialists and missionaries had, he added, alienated the Southern tribespeople from their Northern Arab brothers. The British had left the country but the missionaries remained to deepen the gulf between the South and the North. Were it not for this outside interference, the Sudan would have been a united country. So reasoned the Minister of the Interior.

The Minister listed some of the offenses. Even remote Doro and the missionaries there were included. "It has also been proven that the church at Doro gives facilities to offenders who challenge the law of the land, to leave the country. It happened that one of the cars belonging to that church met with an accident and that some of the passengers died and others were injured. It was also discovered that among the passengers was a prison warder. After inquiry it was clear that the car was on its way to cross the border."

Far to the south of Doro there had been rebellion, violence, and death. Many Southern Sudanese had escaped into neighboring countries. At Doro the missionaries knew of no offenders who had challenged the law. They had not heard of any local Maban tribespeople fleeing from the country into nearby Ethiopia. No mission car had been involved in an accident and the church owned no car. Nobody had died. Nothing was known of a prison warder who had escaped into Ethiopia. None had been aided by missionaries. In fact, there was no road into Ethiopia, thirty miles away. And there had been no inquiry.

So this was the "evidence"! For such reasons the missionaries in the Southern Sudan were being expelled. This was official and this was the end.

2

The Unity of the Nile Valley

✻✖✻✖✻✖✻✖✻✖✻✖✻✖✻✖✻✖✻✖

THE SCANDAL of the Sudan long had been its division into two distinct parts. Many Sudanese, who knew why the division existed, refused to accept the historical explanation. It was easier for them to blame the strife on people close at hand, the missionaries and the recently departed British "imperialists."

It was obvious enough. The dominant religion in the country was Islam. Following the preaching of the Gospel by the missionaries, many Southerners had become Christians. In mission schools, the Christians had tended to adopt Western ways. They became more like the Christians in Uganda than the Sudanese in the North.

Arabic was the natural *lingua franca* of the country. Missionaries taught the Southern people to read and write in their own tribal languages. They taught English. This was the policy handed down to them by the British educators. Later, when it became government policy to teach Arabic, the missionaries gladly complied.

The real truth about the Sudan's divisions was not so obvious. When British administrators and missionaries reached the Sudan early in the twentieth century the country was already deeply and violently divided. Climate, terrain, race, color, and religion all had contributed to this division.

When Turks, Egyptians, and Northern Sudanese began their incursions into the South in search of slaves and ivory, they sowed the seeds of strife that would plague their descendants far into the twentieth century.

To the Egyptians and the Northern Sudanese, the South was hostile territory. They hated its long rainy season with its mosquitoes and mud. There was little rain where they lived. They disliked the people and looked down on them. They were not fellow human beings to be raised to higher levels of existence. They were natural resources, like gold and ivory. The people of the desert Nile did not like the South but they would not let it go.

When the Sudan became an independent country in 1956, it was still divided by this attitude and by the Southern response to it. Most Northern Sudanese administrators and civil servants avoided appointment to the South if they could. Only a handful of government servants loved the South and its people.

Each year when the rainy season ended in the Sudan, nomadic herdsmen from the North followed the water and grass to the South. They turned up with their herds along the southern reaches of the Nile and its tributaries. They often let their sheep and cattle roam through the standing grain of the tribespeople. There were reprisals.

When the rains came again, the nomads moved back

to their northern deserts where their animals grazed on thornbrush and grain stalks. The South was not the home of these people though they spent half of each year there.

When the fifty-days wind began to blow in December, Khartoum and Omdurman merchants loaded their sprawling river boats with salt, sugar, pots and pans, kerosene, beads and wire for bracelets, raised their huge sails to the wind, and disappeared into the southern haze.

They traded their wares for poached ivory, grain, leopard skins, and cow hides. When they had used up all their trade goods, they drifted slowly downstream and returned to the comfort of their mud-walled homes in the desert cities. They had been in a foreign country.

In the South the tribesmen were using and contending with the Nile in their own way. As the level of the river rose and spread over whole counties, turning them into vast swamps, they moved to higher ground with their cattle. They planted fields of millet. They worked hard.

When the waters receded, they followed them with fire, burning off the ten-foot-high elephant grass. In a few weeks the cracked clay soil produced a new crop of rich pasture. Tribesmen moved in with their cattle. In some places they competed for the grass with the roving herdsmen from the North. Northerner and Southerner used the Nile each in his own way. But "one Nile" did not unite them.

If, in the nineteen sixties, there was only one division in the Sudan, that between the North and the South, it was an improvement on the Sudan of the mid-nineteenth century. At that time the people of the far West had their own kingdom. The Northern Sudanese were dominated by their Egyptian-Turkish overlords. The Southern Sudanese were separated from the rest of the country and from each other by a hundred dissimilar languages, endless tribal customs and taboos, and an underlying belief in each tribe that it, in reality, constituted the "world."

When politics came to life in the post World War II Sudan, North and West had already been united. The only serious division in the country was that between the North and South. This became the major factor in the political life of the country.

Outside the country, changes were taking place which would influence the future of the Sudan. In Egypt General Mohammed Neguib and Colonel Gamal Abdel Nasser sent King Farouk into exile. Looking southward they proclaimed for Egypt and the Sudan the "unity of the Nile Valley." There was to be, they said, "one God, one language, one river."

Nasser convinced many Western people, among them some Christians, that Islam was the cementing force that held the peoples of the Middle East and Moslem Africa together. He claimed that the Moslems' belief in the brotherhood of men and its historic repudiation of discrimination because of color and race gave Islam a great advantage over Christians in the quest for the soul of the African.

Nasser was not able to prove his point. His fellow Moslems in the Sudan repudiated "the unity of the Nile Valley." The Northern Sudanese tried to unite their own country not by brotherhood but by political and religious pressure.

Though the Sudanese refused to accept Nasser's offer of the unity of the Nile Valley, their country had been deeply influenced by Egypt for centuries. The Pharaohs and their successors had looked southward with much concern for it was from that direction that the Nile flowed. And the Nile was the life of Egypt.

If unfriendly spirits or people near the unknown sources of the river should dry it up or divert it, it would mean disaster for the Egyptians who were unfamiliar with rain. They did not know from whence the Nile came. About A.D. 150 Ptolemy had sketched a rough map, using his imagination to fill in central Africa.

He showed the Nile coming from the "Mountains of the Moon" which stretched across "Terra Incognita." Not until the end of the eighteenth century did James Bruce reveal the source of the Blue Nile at Lake Tana in Ethiopia. It was much later, in the middle of the nineteenth century, that British explorers—John Speke, James Grant, and Richard Burton among others—discovered and mapped "Terra Incognita" and revealed to the world the existence of a lake second in size to Superior which they called Victoria. They showed that the stream that flowed northward from the lake was the Nile. Later it became known as the White Nile. Ptolemy's map had been amazingly accurate. The "Mountains of the Moon" was the Ruwenzori Range.

Two German missionaries, Johann Krapf and Johann Rebmann, who worked with a British mission on the Kenya coast, discovered snow-capped Kenya and Kilimanjaro. From their equatorial snows the Nile received some of its strength.

The story of Egyptian influence in the Sudan goes back well before 2000 B.C. By that time the Pharaohs had penetrated some fifty miles into the Sudan. They were busy building pyramids and temples. They carved Abu

Simbel out of the solid rock which formed the banks of the Nile just north of the present border between Egypt and the Sudan. Their pyramids can be seen from the train today as it grinds its way across the northern desert.

Egyptian temples tell some of the story of early Sudan history. Their taskmasters are portrayed, lash in hand, raised over the backs of black people who had thick lips and kinky or fuzzy hair.

The Pharaohs faded from the scene as Greek culture and government spread. Greece in turn faded as Rome came to power. Rome's southward interest did not, for a while, penetrate beyond the southern border of Egypt. But within the Empire and out of it events were taking place which would determine the course of the twentieth-century Sudan.

3

✾✖✾✖✾✖✾✖✾✖✾✖✾✖✾✖✾✖✾✖✾✖

The Cross and The Crescent

✾✖✾✖✾✖✾✖✾✖✾✖✾✖✾✖✾✖✾✖✾✖

NEWS traveled slowly in those days, but it traveled, carried by men on foot, on donkeys, and on camels. In Jerusalem strange things had happened where Jew met Roman in a Greek atmosphere. The Romans, encouraged by the Jews, had executed by crucifixion one Jesus who seemed, for a while, to have supernatural powers.

The Romans and the Jews had been thrown into consternation when rumor spread that the dead man had arisen from His grave.

Later His followers had made a cult of these events. They had, in fact, claimed that entrance into the cult would result in a "newness of life" that would transform people regardless of color or race.

This lack of discrimination had nettled both Romans and Jews, and they had turned on the followers of Jesus as they had on Him. Large numbers of Jesus' followers had subsequently been killed. Others had fled and gone everywhere preaching their doctrine.

These new people, who seemed to be at home in any place and with any race, were called "Christians." Their leader, Jesus, had been accepted by believing Jews as the "Anointed One" or Messiah for whom they had been waiting. He was looked upon not so much as a leader but as a Saviour.

Their Saviour had returned to heaven with a promise that He would again visit the earth to complete His mission of saving men and to rule the earth. The story of His life, His sayings, and the doctrinal implications of His life, death, and resurrection were recorded by His followers and eventually brought together as the New Testament.

As the life of Jesus on earth became only a memory, Christians argued over the meaning of His coming. They debated the person of Jesus. The accepted doctrine of the Church was that Jesus was truly God and truly man. These two persons had been perfectly united to form a new being, unlike any previous creature. He was fully God and fully man.

Some theologians of the early centuries refused to accept this doctrine. Jesus was God, they said. His appearance in a body was incidental. He did not become man. Chief promoter of this view was Nestorius of Antioch. A Church council was called in 436 to investigate Nestorius' views. He was declared a heretic and was banished.

Forced to leave Antioch, Nestorius went eastward to get away from the authority of the Church that had repudiated him. Arabia was outside the Roman Empire.

It was also outside the area affected by the work of the Church. Nestorius preached the Gospel there.

In the sixth century Arabia had no national existence. It was made up of a number of independent tribes, some of which were nominally Christian. Some had been influenced by Jews who had fled southward following the massacres that had attended Titus' destruction of Jerusalem in A.D. 70.

Others were pagan. They had a center of worship at a place called Mecca. Certain sacred stones were enshrined there in what the people called the "Kabba."

The people in Arabia claimed descent from Abraham through Ishmael. In the sixth century, Jews, Arabs, and Christians were tolerant of each other. In this era of tolerance, Christianity and Judaism in Arabia had lost much of their meaning and force. Across North Africa the Christian Church flourished.

In this sixth-century Arabia was born a child who was to create the third monotheistic force in the Middle East, Mohammed. He was born about the year 570.

Mohammed lost his father at an early age. He went to live with relatives. He was a dreamer and, in some respects, a sensitive soul. During his youth he was assigned to travel with caravans which wended their way back and forth across the deserts and plains of the Middle East. He visited Syria and traveled through Jordan. He listened to the discussions of current thought around the campfires at night. It was an exciting life.

If Christianity had not lost its first love, Mohammed might have become a Christian. Mohammed in Syria might have become a convert to Jesus Christ through the preaching of Paul or Peter. But nearly five hundred years had passed since their voices had called men to faith in Christ.

Mohammed's relatives noticed that he was given to contemplation. Since their business was flourishing, they permitted him to take time to meditate and to discuss philosophy with religious leaders.

Mohammed was unhappy with the pagan Arabs who spent their time offering sacrifices to the spirits. Theirs was a negative religion.

He became familiar with Jewish and Christian beliefs. Later he was to draw on them heavily in his own writings. Mohammed found no satisfaction in any of the philosophies around him. He began to think along new lines.

He borrowed stories from the Talmud. He included Jesus and the Biblical account of the virgin birth and other New Testament doctrines. Then he added his own ideas. This synthesis was the begining of his religion— Islam.

The Jews did not have to be offended for Mohammed made Jesus a prophet rather than the Son of God. He took Him from the cross and sent Him back to heaven uncrucified. Another was put on the cross in His place.

For Christians Jesus could remain as the greatest prophet up to the time of Mohammed. He would return to earth. When He returned, He would be second in authority to Mohammed. Mohammed did not destroy the pagans nor their Kabba, though he denounced idolatry. He turned the Kabba into a place of Moslem worship. Eventually it became the object of pilgrims from all over the world.

With his "something for everybody" Mohammed was

able to woo the peoples of Arabia. Christians, whose faith had lapsed, joined him. The Jews remained faithful to their religion.

Mohammed promoted Islam as the true successor to Judaism and Christianity. Christianity, he said, was a good but incomplete revelation of the will of God. It must accept the final authority of Islam.

Mohammed denounced what he called the polytheism of the Christians. God was one, he said. Jesus could not be God. "God was not born, neither does He give birth," he wrote. The Christian doctrine that declared Jesus to be the Son of God was the one most severely attacked by Mohammed.

The new prophet had to have some authority for what he was doing. He withdrew to the desert where, he said, God gave to him copies of His writings. Mohammed's copies were then introduced to his followers as "The Koran." There could be no errors in the Koran. It was merely a copy of the words of God written in heaven.

As Mohammed's movement grew, he added compulsion to persuasion. Islam burst out of its homeland and crossed Egypt and North Africa. Strong churches on the southern coast of the Mediterranean ceased to exist. Then Islam turned eastward and swallowed up the Mesopotamian Valley and Persia. It crossed India, stopping long enough to become one of the principal religions there. It went on to Afghanistan and China. But for the moment it failed to penetrate one of its nearest neighbors, the Sudan.

Before the advent of Islam, Egypt's chief religion was Christianity. Christian communities with their churches were established along the Nile. Alexandria became one of the chief cities of Empire and church. Missionaries from that seat of religious authority went on preaching missions up the Nile by camel and slow boat.

When they settled among the Nubians on both sides of the Sudan-Egyptian border, they reduced the language of the people to writing and taught them to read the Bible.

The Northern Sudan was then divided into three kingdoms. The southernmost, called Alwa, had its capital at Soba, near present-day Khartoum. Evangelists from Egypt penetrated the entire area. By the time Islam was born in Arabia, much of the Northern Sudan was Christian.

After the Moslems had conquered Egypt and North Africa, they turned southward toward Nubia. They sent expeditions against the Christians in the Sudan but these were defeated by the people who were experts in the use of bow and arrow.

The first serious penetration of the Arabs came in 651. They were not able to defeat the Sudanese finally. A compromise was reached. The Sudanese agreed to supply 350 choice slaves per year to the Arab invaders. They also agreed to return runaway slaves, to protect Arab travelers, and to respect the mosques that were erected for those who became Moslems. This agreement was the first step in the ultimate extinction of Christianity in the Sudan.

The 350 "choice" slaves had to be produced from somewhere. Merchants in Nubia had connections with dealers who operated far to the south where African tribespeople had become the raw materials of a new industry.

To secure the raw materials, raiders entered villages by night. They killed the men who resisted. They captured women and children and submissive men, put them in chains, and started them off on the long journey to "civilization." With the blood of these captives peace was maintained between the Arabs and the Nubians.

During the six hundred years of this peace, pressure from the north increased. By the sixteenth century, only Alwa survived as a Christian kingdom in the Sudan. Its religion was not indigenous. The Church depended on the Patriarchate in Alexandria to supply priests. And Alexandria was twelve hundred miles from Khartoum. The Arabs made it difficult for priests to make the journey to Alwa. The churches there went without services for long periods.

The Gospels had been translated into the Nubian language. No translation work had taken place in Alwa. The Alexandrian priests used only the ancient, dead Coptic language. Their services consisted of ritual: endless repetitions and the burning of incense. The Christianity Paul had preached in the known world had become, at Alwa, a dead form. This form of Christianity had no roots in the Sudan. Its roots were in Alexandria. It was a foreign religion.

In the meantime Arab-Egyptian-Moslem penetration continued. These people were not in a hurry. Arabs married local women. Their offspring became chiefs and leaders. Being sons of local women they were not foreigners. They spoke the local languages well.

The Arabs with their religion promoted a way of life which was sensual. Any spiritual force was mystical and had to accommodate itself to the practical. Christianity was a spiritual force which could succeed only when it was allowed to dominate the lives of those who received it. Backsliding brought weakness throughout the family of believers. Islam survived as a way of life no matter how carnal its people became.

Christianity in the Kingdom of Alwa could survive only if it were a spiritual force. This it was not. Islam increased its religious, military, economic, and cultural pressure against it. The Christianity of Alwa was not worth defending. The people capitulated and Islam took over. A few minutes' drive now takes curious people from Khartoum to Soba where they can poke in the ruins of one of the churches. Little remains.

Three centuries passed before representatives of a Christian church appeared in the Sudan. They were Roman Catholics, members of The Society for the Propagation of the Faith. The leaders of this society had heard that a way into Central Africa was being opened up on the Nile. Haste to use this new route was necessary as it was rumored that some Protestants were planning to proclaim their doctrine somewhere up the River. Furthermore the followers of Mohammed were in the area in force.

This was the background that led Pope Gregory XVI to announce in 1846 the formation of the Vicariate Apostolic of Central Africa. The first missionaries—Polish, Slovene, and Italian—reached Khartoum in February, 1848. Roman Catholics have never carried on much work aimed at winning Moslems to Christianity. The first Catholic missionaries in the Sudan intended to reach the tribespeople.

The slave trade, the warfare between Arabs and tribespeople and between the tribes themselves, the impossible conditions of rain, mud, and mosquitoes, and the unwillingness of the people to sell their grain—all these made the establishment of mission stations hazardous. There were repeated attempts to settle missionaries in towns and villages along the Nile but there was to be no more peace for the priests than there was for the Arabs and the tribespeople.

Even in the heart of Africa in the midst of warfare, brutality, and insecurity, Rome's lack of appreciation of the doctrine of the separation of church and state was apparent. Priests, hoping to establish a station by winning the friendship of a chief, heard that he was troubled by attacks from his rival. The priests agreed to supply him with firearms.

Knoblecher, an Austrian, was one of the first priests to attempt work in Equatoria. When he saw the impossibility of doing anything in an area that had no law, he went to his homeland and appealed to Emperor Franz Josef to establish a consular service in Khartoum. The service was to include the "protection of the Catholic Mission."

The Austrian Emperor sent a representative to the Sudan. Khartoum, a city of mud houses surrounded by grass or mud walls, simmered on the dry sands which formed the tongue of land between the Blue and White Niles. In 1830 the Egyptian Governor General of the Sudan had established Khartoum as his capital.

The land along the river banks was irrigated by Persian water wheels which had been introduced by the Egyptians. The farmers produced grain and vegetables;

they grew fodder for their animals. Khartoum was greatly inferior to Cairo but there were amenities.

Merchants and explorers equipped themselves in the town's shops before moving upstream to carry on their work.

Once the merchants and missionaries left Khartoum, the Austrian consul was able to do little for them.

In the South the priests often found themselves working with merchants whose activities were on traditional lines. Their affairs became involved with those of adventurers who were Catholics in name only. The priests and merchants often had common interests. Such a common interest would be rejected by many Protestants and Catholics. The local people would see nothing strange in this relationship. The Arabs in their midst had never separated their religion from their commercial interests.

The Austrian missionaries established stations and then were forced to abandon them. Their trade goods were stolen. Stations deteriorated and were closed. Others were opened where, it was hoped, the people would learn to trade with the missionaries if nothing more. Before they could preach their religion, the priests had to survive. They abandoned some of their centers without having had any influence on the lives of the village people.

On the upper Nile all foreigners—Arabs and Turks, Europeans, and Northern Sudanese—were suspect. To make progress, the missionaries had to be known for their peculiar work. But they were forced to get goods they needed by trading with beads. Their servants engaged in a similar trade. In this confusion, the tribespeople saw no reason to treat the priests as anything but merchants.

The fortunes of the Roman Catholic missions rose and fell between the opening of the work in 1848 and its end in 1871. The lack of stable government, the terror of the slave trade, and the deadly climate had proved too much even for missionaries. They left the Southern Sudan as they had found it. There was no peace. There was scarcely a convert. As for the Protestants, they had not yet appeared on the scene.

4

The Turks on the Nile

THE TURKS had been the first white-skinned people to investigate the area along the Sudan-Ethiopian border where we were to live. Their presence in the Sudan was the result of changes that had taken place in Egypt. Mohammed Aly, a Turkish adventurer, had taken over as Khedive in Cairo.

When we arrived in the Central Sudan in 1939 to begin our work, we were surprised to be addressed as "Turuks." We were amused and perhaps a little resentful. In our lifetime we had heard such expressions as "the unspeakable Turk" and we remembered the massacre of Armenian Christians in Turkey. And we were Turks.

The first Turkish ruler in Egypt, Mohammed Aly, was born in 1769. He was wily and ruthless. By cunning he quickly eliminated all competition. He became master in the land.

Mohammed Aly organized the country according to his own designs. The peasants along the River were taxed;

their grain was taken for the feeding of the army. Businessmen in the cities were kept in line by the Turkish garrisons which were established everywhere.

With Egypt in his control, Mohammed began to investigate the Sudan. Tales of unlimited numbers of tribespeople and rich gold mines came to him as they had come to the many rulers who had preceded him in Cairo.

Like his predecessors, Mohammed Aly was conscious of the annual rise and fall of the River. Bruce had found the reservoir of the Blue Nile, Lake Tana in northern Ethiopia and its junction with the White Nile at Khartoum was known. The flood had been partially accounted for. Flowing silently out of the papyrus swamps of the Sudan, the White Nile was still a mystery, giving not a hint of its past as it glided through the changeless "land of the blacks."

Mohammed Aly had to look to his affairs with considerable concentration. As he had filled a political vacuum, so some new interloper would fill any vacuum he allowed to develop as a result of his inaction.

Mohammed had been carried to power in Egypt on the shoulders of his Albanian and Turkish soldiers. They would not be content to live in barracks, to be restricted to their monthly pay, or to be left out of the mainstream of political life. To them soldiering had always meant attack, loot, and a period of enjoying the fruits of their depredations. They needed new fields to conquer. If Mohammed Aly did not concern himself with their interests, they might cause him serious trouble.

He could divert the attention of his soldiers easily with the promise of wealth to be obtained by an expedition of conquest and pillage up the Nile.

The Nile also attracted the explorer and the anti-

quarian. The search for gold and slaves drew the sol-
dier-adventurer. All found themselves pushing together
over the hot sands along the Nile. The slave merchant
was suspicious of the explorer. He was never completely
able to stifle his conscience on selling men and women
as he sold animals. The presence of outsiders, especially
Europeans, irritated him. They were the greatest threat
to the security of his traffic.

When they reached the Moslem slave markets in the
Northern Sudan, black African men were circumcised
and given Moslem names. Some of these, surrendering
hopelessly to the inevitable, became more fanatic in their
new religion than their captors. Now and then a European Christian-turned-Moslem wandered in to study the
land and the ruins of the Pharaohs and the early Christians.

In the insecure world of the early nineteenth century
Mohammed Aly had to make a decision. He appointed
his son, Ismael, to be the commander of the army that
was to add the Sudan to his country and turn some of
the profits from the slave trade into his own coffers. This
was a big assignment for a young man of twenty-five.
As a prince in Egypt he was said to be well mannered,
soft spoken, and informed about the affairs of his father's
realm.

As the leader of a motley army of four thousand op-
portunists, he was cruel, demanding, cunning, and primitive. His own father, hearing of his son's excesses,
warned him against displays of brutality. Yet Mohammed
could hardly point to his own past in admonishing his
son. The early history of father and son was unhappily
alike.

The Turks and Albanians who were the core of Ismael's

force marched southward to enrich themselves while adding to the Khedive's territory. Mohammed Aly's share was to be forty thousand slaves annually.

Ismael's men might have met with disaster were it not for their guns. The Sudanese tribes they encountered in the North were excellent swordsmen. But this skill was no longer enough. They were slain on the sands before they could get close enough to the invader to use their swords. Resistance crumbled and Ismael and his men had an open road to the junction of the Blue and White Niles.

They continued their march up the Blue Nile to Sennar, breadbasket of the Sudan, and spent the rainy season there. They were not far from the gold mines. When the rains ended in October, they resumed their march up the river. When they finally reached the gold country, they were near the border of Ethiopia where the Blue Nile rolls into the Sudan. Now there is a dam not far away at Roseires.

There was little gold to be found. The stories of productive mines along the border had grown as they reached Khartoum and Cairo. It was a bitter disappointment to Ismael to learn that they were only stories. He began to think of home. The ragged army began its long journey northward. Before they left the area, the soldiers raided tribal villages and took captive women and children.

As Ismael withdrew, he left garrisons scattered throughout the Sudan. In Khartoum he installed a governor-general. The garrison commanders were responsible to him. But they set themselves up as local rulers and exploited the land and the people around them.

They paid the authorities in Khartoum only a token of their gain. The Turks had conquered the Sudan and had made it an Egyptian colony, but they brought no peace to the people.

The Sudan was an Egyptian colony. Egypt was a Turkish protectorate. Britain kept her representatives in Cairo for her financial stake in the country was great. Egyptian rulers tended to spend state funds until there was nothing left with which to pay interest to the British and Continental creditors.

The rulers in Cairo were pressed by these creditors. The revenue they hoped to receive from the Sudan to help them in their extremity failed to reach them. Changing governors-general in Khartoum had never improved the situation. Governors appointed to Equatoria had, one after the other, become partners to the predatory interests there.

Mohammed Aly had passed from the scene in Cairo. The new Khedive was his grandson Ismael. This new ruler had an idea. It came to him as he attended the grand ball that marked the opening of the Suez Canal in 1869 as he faced the old question, "Who can govern Equatoria for Egypt?"

The Canal celebration was one of the most magnificent events Egypt had ever seen or has since known. Royalty was there from several European countries. Engineers, businessmen, and statesmen flocked to Cairo and Port Said by the thousands.

Among those who attended the grand opening were Sir Samuel and Lady Baker. This was not their first visit to Africa. They had already explored the headwaters of the Nile, had discovered a lake which they named Albert after the late Prince Consort. They had wandered through central Africa for five years, often more dead than alive.

At the Suez celebration, which Sir Samuel attended as an interpreter, Ismael called Baker aside. He asked him to accept appointment as Governor of Equatoria.

Heretofore all the Egyptian representatives in the Southern Sudan had become involved in the corruption and raiding that marked life there. Ismael asked Sir Samuel to lead an expedition which, under his strong hand, would not become involved, as had previous expeditions, in the very traffic they were to end.

Ismael stood between the Europe on which he was dependent for financial help and the Sudan where conditions existed which made Europeans reluctant to help him. European and British financiers did not want a matter such as slavery to interfere with their operations. But the success of their business depended on the good will of the public in Europe and Britain and that public was asking embarrassing questions about the conditions that existed from Egypt to Zanzibar and Arabia.

Sir Samuel's assignment was to include an attempt to bring the kingdoms of Uganda into the Turko-Egyptian Empire. Apparently neither Sir Samuel nor others of his kind in Victorian England or on the continent saw anything strange or inconsistent about promoting the expansionism of a country in the Middle East and a corrupt one at that.

Sir Samuel Baker agreed to undertake the task of establishing some kind of order on the Nile. He agreed to extend Egyptian civilization unto the unclaimed portions of Africa as far as Zanzibar and including Ethiopia, if possible.

To carry out his expedition Sir Samuel had to have an army and a corps of technicians. Cairo was not lacking in foreigners waiting to be hired for such an expedition. Their presence in the Egyptian capital indicated that they had the necessary spirit of adventure (if they weren't running away from the hard realities of life) but it did not indicate that they would be useful to a civilizing expedition. From them Baker chose his staff.

Ismael provided the army of Sudanese and Egyptians. Some were even released from prison and assigned to Baker. Many were criminals.

It took Baker months to break through the papyrus growth on the Nile far south of Khartoum. He could have perished in the vegetation which, animal-like, was capable of destroying marooned men. When at last he broke through into clear water, he was anything but a conquering hero. He was exhausted and his men were in a state of collapse. His first act in Equatoria showed the anomaly of his position. In the depths of the Nile swamps he rededicated the emptiness and hopelessness of Gondokoro not to Ismael and his Egyptian government but to the Ottoman Empire which, in the upside-down world of Baker, was the real owner of his contract. Baker stood before his troops and solemnly raised the Ottoman flag. Gondokoro was one of few names known in Equatoria. It was a place. But when Baker or his predecessors were not there, it was nothing.

Sir Samuel established garrisons; he fought the king

of Buganda but could not subdue him. In the end he left Equatoria not much better than he found it. Nothing was added to the Khedive's empire.

Ismael would have to find another mercenary to mount another expedition to Equatoria. This expedition would have to go through all the motions again.

Baker was to have a hand in the appointment of a successor. In London he met a rising star of empire and glory, General Charles Gordon. The meeting was fateful for Gordon. He would have much work to do before he, like Baker, looked out upon a land he was finally unable to help or subdue.

5

※※※※※※※※※※※※※※※※※※

Gordon of Khartoum

※※※※※※※※※※※※※※※※※※

GORDON was no novice. He had already had a large part in suppressing the Taiping rebellion in China. He had served in the Crimea. The son of a British Army officer, he had known little but army life as a child and as an adult.

Gordon served under three different appointments in the Sudan. He first served as Governor of Equatoria Province in the far south. His duties were to bring order out of chaos, to control if not to wipe out the slave trade, and to impose Egyptian authority upon Arab leaders who were ruling each in his sovereign territory.

Gordon completed Baker's unfinished exploration of the course of the White Nile from the Sudan to Lake Victoria. He did not have administrative nor military power to take and to hold the kingdoms north of the lakes so after exploring the area he withdrew to his own headquarters in the swamp. Gordon's province was a happier place than it had been under any of his predecessors.

But this was not enough. His assignment had included the pushing of the Sudan frontier all the way to Lake Victoria. In this he had failed.

Plagued by his own sense of failure, overcome with the enormity of the task of bringing enduring order out of the Equatorial chaos, Gordon made his way down the Nile to Cairo. His contract had expired.

Ismael begged Gordon to accept reappointment to the governorship of Equatoria. But Gordon had had enough. He returned to Britain. There he wrote his letter of resignation and sent it to Cairo. The year 1876 was coming to a close. Gordon, discouraged with his failures, was through with Africa.

But Ismael was not through with Gordon. The Sudan was still the Khedive's greatest anxiety. Embarrassing questions were always being asked in Cairo. In that city there was not one person Ismael could trust with his Sudan affairs.

Ismael sent a telegram to Gordon in London. Gordon was in a favorable bargaining position. He would return only if he were made governor-general of the whole Sudan with almost unlimited powers. Ismael accepted Gordon's terms.

The appointment put new life into Gordon. He entered his territory via the Red Sea coast in May 1877. He reached Khartoum by camel across hundreds of miles of desert and thus began the legend that was to mark him for the remainder of his life and beyond. It was a true legend for Gordon crossed and recrossed the Sudan by camel, turning up unexpectedly to inspect the work of government servants, moving so rapidly that he outstripped all warnings of his arrival. He was, up to his time, the best informed governor-general of the Sudan.

As governor-general he had a work to do. He had inherited an administration that was corrupt down to the last messenger boy. To support the corruption such heavy taxes, fees, and levies had been placed on the farmers and merchants that they could no longer survive. Merchants had gone out of business. Farmers had left their water wheels.

Gordon moved quickly. He dismissed Egyptian and Arab officials by the score. He replaced them with Sudanese and Europeans. Farmers and merchants began to see that there was hope after all. They returned to their work. Conditions improved for all classes of people. Reasonable taxes and rates brought into the treasury more money than extortion had done under Gordon's predecessors.

Gordon's success inevitably produced enemies. He was an infidel ruling over Moslems. He was the despoiler of merchants who had grown rich on the slave trade. He had brought all activity within the bounds of legitimacy. Those who had gotten rich with their activities outside these bounds were furious. This puritanical form of government was not for them.

Gordon had received his appointment as governor-general of the Sudan from Ismael Pasha, Khedive of Egypt. Ismael was removed from his office by the order of the Khedive in Constantinople. His son Taufik had replaced him. Gordon's strongest link with Egypt was broken.

He read his Bible and meditated. He fretted over

his position and about almost everything else in the world. Khartoum was no place for a melancholy governor-general. He resigned.

With Gordon gone, the Khedive began his search for another governor-general. He had neither time nor inclination to give the appointment much thought. The British had landed a force at Suez and had moved inland. The Khedive had fled to Alexandria. When he returned to Cairo, it was to continue as ruler under the authority of Sir Evelyn Baring. In the confused relationships of the day, Britain became master of Egypt and then insisted that Egypt be responsible for the administration of the Sudan.

With an understandable lack of concern, Taufik appointed Raouf Pasha to serve as governor-general in Khartoum. Gordon had once dismissed this man for corruption and for cruelty to the Sudanese.

Gordon had managed to bring some order out of chaos in the Sudan. When Raouf arrived in Khartoum chaos was already returning to the Sudan. Raouf's partners in maladministration were waiting to join him. Soon the Sudanese were back where Gordon had found them. The Egyptians reimposed the land taxes, the water taxes, sales taxes, and purchase taxes. Sudanese who failed to pay sufficient of their income to the authorities were lashed with the ever-present hippo hide *kourbash*.

In the South, the tribespeople who had enjoyed respite under Gordon found themselves the victims of the new maladministration. They moved deeper into the swamps. Their goal was survival.

The next flicker of hope in the Northern Sudan came

not with a foreigner hired by a khedive but from a Sudanese religious man. He had moved from the big bend in the Nile just south of Egypt to the environs of Omdurman as the son of a boat builder. His name was, of course, Mohammed. Officially he was Mohammed Achmed Abdallah.

He was inclined toward religion and study. Since his three brothers could carry on their father's business, he was permitted to follow his pious inclinations.

He studied at various religious schools where he memorized the Koran and learned to read and write. The religious leaders who taught him marked him as one to follow them in their profession.

Having given himself to the study and recital of the Koran, Mohammed took the next step of devotion. He left his fellow devotees and took up a lonely life on Aba Island, in the White Nile some one hundred and sixty miles south of Khartoum.

He was not alone long. A Moslem holy man must have followers. His learning and devotion attracted attention. Men gathered around him to listen to his preaching. Inevitably rumor spread that this man had prophetic dreams and unusual powers. Mohammed did not deny these attributions.

Among those who attached themselves to the rising prophet was a searcher from the west, Abdallahi. Abdallahi's father had been a religious teacher and prophet. He had urged his son to seek for the leader who would doubtless arise within Islam. Abdallahi, the son, heard rumors of the prophet of Aba Island and he presented himself as a follower.

A movement had begun. It had to have a purpose and

direction. Moslem eschatology included a belief that a guide, a leader would come to restore Islam to its place of purity and leadership. The doctrine was not precise and so lent itself to a variety of situations. Mohammed Achmed allowed the belief to grow that he was the promised guide. His followers began to speak of him as the Mahdi, the Messiah. He was 34. The year was 1881.

As word of this new development traveled, Sudanese Moslems made their way in increasing numbers to the Mahdi's center. Most of these were farmers whose superstition was as great as their religious devotion. It was not likely that they would ask the Mahdi any difficult questions about his dreams and doctrine.

Every prophet, reformer, or crusader must have a cause. The Mahdi did not have far to look for one. Under the domination of Egypt, the practice of orthodox Islam in the Sudan had languished. Through their confiscatory taxation, slave dealing, and corruption Egyptian Moslems dishonored their religion. With the example of the Egyptians and their own loss of initiative in religion and life, the Sudanese were following the Koran afar off. The Mahdi called for a return to true worship and life.

Raouf Pasha, the governor-general in Khartoum, knew that such a pious movement as the Mahdi had begun could turn out to be a rebellion against his authority. He sent a delegation of learned men to the Mahdi's island retreat to persuade him to give up his claims. But the Mahdi's movement was already showing signs of success and his followers would not bow again to Egyptian authority.

Many Sudanese had journeyed to Aba Island to investigate the rumors they had heard about the Mahdi. Now the Mahdi proclaimed himself as the Messiah that was to come. He invited all men to join him.

The governor-general in Khartoum became alarmed. It was evident that an expedition must be sent to capture the Mahdi and to end the threat of insurrection. Raouf sent a detachment of soldiers to bring the rebel leader to him.

Neither the governor-general nor his soldiers had yet taken the Mahdi seriously. He and his followers, they believed, were simple, rural people. They had no firearms. They had only sticks and spears. A few men with rifles could overcome them.

The soldiers decided to go ashore from their boats at night. That was a fatal mistake. In the darkness the men could not see their targets. The Mahdi's followers, with their religious fervor and their faith in the divine appointment of their leader, attacked the invaders in the darkness. Only a few Egyptians escaped into the river and to the waiting boats. The Jehad, the holy war, was on.

This was to be a strange holy war. The term was usually applied to Moslem attacks on infidel Christians. In the new Jehad the Mahdi was to fight fellow Moslems. It was not religious enmity that led to this crusade. It was the oppression and the cruelty of the Egyptians that gave rise to the Mahdi's rebellion. But he called it a Jehad.

The religious leader now became known as a military genius. Though he was attacked by superior forces, he won battle after battle. There was only one way his followers could explain his successes. God was with him.

The Mahdi was now a rebel. He could no longer sit on his island welcoming pilgrims from all over the Sudan. He moved to the safety of the western Nuba Hills.

El Obeid with its Egyptian garrison was the first large city to which he laid siege. The city was some three hundred miles southwest of Khartoum. The Mahdi's men sealed off El Obeid from the surrounding country. The inhabitants believed that help would certainly come. While they waited, food supplies dwindled. Prices went up. Coffee sold for twenty dollars a pound. The price of a chicken was thirty dollars. Salt cost a dollar an ounce.

As the end of the siege neared, all livestock had been consumed. Once-rich people were reduced to eating mice, dogs, crickets, and cockroaches. People died in large numbers and their bodies littered the streets. Resistance had lost its meaning. The garrison capitulated. With the capture of El Obeid and its troops, the Mahdi's prestige greatly increased.

It is doubtful that the Mahdi had any "master plan" for the defeat of the Egyptians and the setting up of an independent Sudanese government when he began his life as a prophet. But he could not stop at El Obeid. Armies were still being sent against him from Khartoum. He would march on Khartoum itself and bring to an end the sin and the injustice of Egyptian rule.

The Mahdi was on the march! If he had no long-range plans when he left Aba Island, he had them now. He was on his way to Khartoum. Gladstone, the British prime minister, and Queen Victoria reacted in London. The khedive reacted in Cairo. The Egyptian governor-general reacted in Khartoum. The reactions and the inability of the British and Egyptian officials to define authority in the Sudan crisis led to a long series of ineptitudes that ended in the governor-general's palace in Khartoum.

Britain had sent her troops into Egypt and was in control there. But she insisted that Egypt was responsible for maintaining order in the Sudan. Sir Evelyn Baring was Her Majesty's proconsul in Cairo. He, more than any other, knew what was going on in Egypt and the Sudan. Yet his dispatches to London were misinterpreted or ignored.

The Mahdi's advance had changed the Egyptian approach to the Sudan issue. The question had been, "How can Egypt retain control of the Sudan?" Now it was, "How can Egyptian troops be rescued from certain annihilation in the Sudan?"

All Baring needed was authority from London to do something. This authority was never given.

He requested that some high-ranking British officer be sent to the Sudan to withdraw all the Egyptian garrisons and, if possible, to leave some kind of administration to carry on. What would happen to the thousands of Egyptian civilians, including women and children, was not clear.

Under the most favorable circumstances it would have taken a year to move them to Egypt. The circumstances under which such an evacuation would have to take place now would be decidedly unfavorable. The Mahdi would take advantage of the withdrawal to harass and to destroy. The Egyptians had dishonored the true faith and he would be doing the will of Allah in destroying them.

Gladstone ignored Baring's request for a high-ranking British officer. But the British newspapers did not. All

Baring needed was one man. In his country's hour of crisis it was difficult to find that man. The Sudan question produced a crisis in the British cabinet. It was the newspapers that finally produced a brilliant suggestion: "Send General Gordon."

In London the newspapers wrote, "If Gordon believes he can use his personal influence in Khartoum . . ." That was the trouble. It was not Gordon's ability as a military man that was being recommended. It was his personal influence. To Baring this was neither good diplomacy nor good military strategy.

The decision concerning Gordon was not made in Cairo. It was made in London. Gladstone agreed to appoint Gordon. This brought an end, for the present, to the cabinet crisis. What Gordon was to do when he reached Khartoum was not clear. After meeting with the cabinet, Gordon stated that he was assigned to evacuate Egyptian troops and civilians from the Sudan. The cabinet ministers replied that his one duty was to go to Khartoum merely to report on the situation there. It was never clear whether he was to report or to organize evacuation. In Khartoum the time for giving advice and for reporting was past.

If the members of the cabinet in London and Baring in Cairo had misgivings about Gordon's mission, the general had none. On his way to Cairo he wrote out the proclamations he would make on his arrival in Khartoum. He knew that the Sudanese had rebelled against Egyptian authority because of the years of oppression. He would respond to this feeling by appointing local Sudanese chiefs to replace the Egyptians.

Gordon would proclaim the end of exploitation. Thus

there would be no reason for the Mahdi's rebellion to proceed further. As he wrote out his proclamations, Gordon was unaware of the enormity of the changes that had taken place in the Sudan since his departure.

Egyptian misrule was already being dealt with—by the Mahdi. Tribal leaders had already been delivered from Egyptian corruption and had been given status— by the Mahdi. The Sudan was rapidly achieving independence—through the Mahdi. Gordon would have nothing to offer.

When he reached Khartoum Gordon did make his offers. He appointed the Mahdi sultan of Kordofan and sent word of the appointment together with new robes suitable for his office. But by this time the Dervish leader was well on his way to becoming sultan of the whole Sudan.

In Khartoum, Gordon soon realized that evacuation was the only answer to the Mahdi's growing threat. Yet he could not resist considering the hope that he, with the help of a small British force, could end the Mahdist threat. Gordon asked the British government for help. The fears of the cabinet ministers were confirmed. Gordon had been sent on his mission to report or at the most to evacuate Egyptian troops. Now he was asking for troops to destroy the Mahdi's forces. As long as Gordon and the cabinet in London continued to misunderstand each other, the Sudan danger would grow. And that misunderstanding would continue to the end.

In London Gladstone told Parliament that Gordon would be permitted to remain in Khartoum until he had fulfilled his assignment. If he believed withdrawal was necessary, he would be free to withdraw.

Gladstone's condescension notwithstanding, it was no longer possible for Gordon to complete his mission or to withdraw. He was trapped. While Gladstone fiddled in London, Gordon burned in Khartoum.

The Mahdi continued his march. There was nothing between him and the River. His armies swarmed over every bit of local resistance. The Egyptian garrisons fell one after the other. Each triumph brought him more guns, ammunition, grain, and volunteers.

Expeditions continued their attempts to move southward across the desert from Egypt to rescue Gordon and his men. The general sent repeated requests for help. "Send me a small detachment. Send me three thousand Turks and I will quickly put down this uprising."

Troop travel south of Egypt was slow and difficult. The Nile was plagued with cataracts. Gunboats could ascend the river only when pulled by thousands of men manning long ropes. The desert sands along the Nile were soft and wearing on men. The desert mountains between Egypt and the Sudan confined all travel to slow river boats.

Gordon stood on the flat roof of his palace hoping to see the first trace of smoke from the gunboats of the relief expedition. He did not know that his would-be deliverers were struggling across the desert or up the river far from his besieged fort.

In March 1884 the Mahdi's forces reached Khartoum and began their siege. They took the mud-walled city of Omdurman across the main Nile. They looked across the Blue Nile to Gordon's palace. Time was on their side. The rivers which had provided security for Gordon on two sides were falling. The White Nile was soon a shallow stream. The Dervishes would be able to wade across it.

Khartoum was suffering in the siege. Food supplies were gone. The inhabitants ate the remaining chickens, donkeys, and vegetation. Then there was nothing left. The dead lay in the streets.

The Dervishes had Khartoum tightly sealed. Deserters left the city and gave the Mahdi fresh reports on conditions inside the walls. The Mahdi's men watched the falling Nile. They made their plans for the final attack.

From his palace roof Gordon could see increased activity on the River. The Mahdi was planning another move. Gordon rallied his forces to one last effort of watchfulness and defense.

The sun set in the desert across the White Nile ending the twenty-fifth day of January 1885. The moon was dark. The River was low. Before dawn on the twenty-sixth, the Mahdi and three of his emirs crossed the White Nile with their troops. He gave instructions and closed with the words, "Do not kill Gordon. Bring him to me." The blessing of Allah was invoked.

The Mahdi's men moved forward stealthily in the pre-dawn darkness. Men on horses followed, ready to back up the infantry wherever they were needed.

Suddenly the Dervishes let loose with guns and rifles. They broke through the defenses. Gordon's hungry men could put up little resistance. Their positions were quickly overrun.

One man above all others was the embodiment of the opposition to the Mahdi. He was somewhere in the darkness. A detachment of soldiers ran to the palace. Acting on their own, they mounted the long stairway. At the top they were confronted by the general. He was dressed in his uniform, waiting for them. The Dervishes attacked him with spears. Knives hacked at him. His head was severed. Khartoum had fallen. General Gordon of Khartoum was dead.

His slayers carried his head to their commander. He was angry. His final instructions to his men had been disobeyed. Perhaps he had hoped to convert the general to Islam. Perhaps it was as well for the Mahdi that Gordon was gone.

6

The Years Between

✳✳✳✳✳✳✳✳✳✳✳✳✳✳✳✳✳✳

GORDON was gone. The war was over. What the Mahdi believed to be God-given victory had swept his forces to unquestioned domination of the Sudan.

The Mahdi had been at war for four years. Large numbers of farmers had left their fields to join his crusade. He had confiscated the grain of those who did plant. Trade had suffered in the midst of war. Thousands of able-bodied men had been killed even through the days of victory. Disease had taken many more. The Mahdi had won the war. Could he win the peace?

This question was never answered for some four months after the death of Gordon, the Mahdi himself was dead. His successor, the Khalifa Abdallahi, had been trained as second in command to the Mahdi. He now took over the affairs of the Dervish Sudan. So victorious an army as that of the Dervishes might do well to push the Egyptians far into their own country, taking control of parts of it. But the Kahlifa soon realized that he had work to do at home. A few Egyptian garrisons still held out in the Sudan. They had been under severe conditions of siege for months. The Kahlifa's forces soon overran them.

During the Mahdi's rise to power, the tribes in the swamps and bushlands of the South were ignored. The European governors Gordon had appointed there continued to administer their provinces though their supplies of arms, ammunition, and food dwindled to nothing. They were able to keep alive with local produce they bought or confiscated.

When the Europeans were finally forced to withdraw, the South lay without administration. The Belgians and the French probed its frontiers. The Khalifa was too busy to investigate, much less administer the area.

The British in Cairo and in London continued to debate the Sudan question. Whatever else they might decide, they had to protect Egypt from invasion by the Khalifa's still fanatic forces. The latter were determined to deal with their former oppressors. They remembered the easy defeats dealt the Egyptians and the British during the rise of the Mahdi. The British, undisciplined and without the driving force of the true religion, would collapse before the onslaught of the disciplined disciples of Islam.

But the day of irregular forces was passing. In Egypt the British had fresh and eager forces of well-trained artillery and cavalry. Gunboats with devastating firepower moved up and down the Nile, on both sides of the Sudan-Egyptian border.

Unaware of the strength of the new British-Egyptian forces, the Dervishes marched northward. Their leaders fervently believed that their past victories were due to the intervention of God as much as to the success of their own arms. They expected Allah to help them to do the impossible again.

But Allah was not noticeably with them. They had fought battles of lesser importance using forty to sixty thousand men. Now they marched against Egypt with five thousand. Their progress was hindered by the thousands of their own camp followers, mostly wives and children, who had to be fed and helped on the way. And it was the hottest time of the year. The sun burned them from the sky. The desert threw the heat back at them from beneath their feet.

When the armies clashed near the Sudan-Egyptian border, the followers of the Mahdi were wiped out. Leading the Anglo-Egyptian cavalry charge was Colonel Kitchener.

The peak of Dervish power and success was passing. The tribes in the South had not been brought under the Khalifa's control. In the North famine and disease were proving to be more deadly than British and Egyptian guns. The Dervishes, glorious in war, did not know how to organize the peace. Religious devotion and fanaticism, which had had a large part in victory, now lapsed.

There had been changes in London and in Cairo also. Gladstone's government had fallen and Lord Salisbury had taken over for the Conservatives. With a new government, all policies of the former administration were reviewed. Sir Evelyn Baring, now Lord Cromer, was more than ever the British presence in Cairo. Officially Britain's control over Egypt was informal and tenuous. In fact Cromer had firm control over all departments of the

Egyptian government. The khedives, prime ministers, and department heads who opposed him had to resign. Cromer carried on.

In Britain idealism survived all changes of government. Lord Salisbury inherited the ghost of Gordon from Gladstone. The British people could not forget the ignominious death of their hero in Khartoum. It was widely believed that ineptitude in London was to blame for Gordon's death and the loss of the Sudan.

In the meantime, new factors entered into British thinking. Italy began her takeover of Eritrea on the eastern border of the Sudan with the capture of Massawa in 1885. She later took the important Sudan town of Kassala from the Khalifa.

King Leopold of the Belgians took possession of a vast area of land on the Congo River. In 1894 the British recognized this seizure as a personal possession of the Belgian King. This put the Belgians in a position to threaten the unadministered southern provinces of the Sudan.

The French had actually occupied some of the Sudan from the west. Later it was to be revealed that General Marchand was under orders to occupy territory all the way to the White Nile.

Britain could wait twenty-five years to vindicate Gordon. She could not wait that long to meet the threat of Italian, Belgian, and French occupation of parts of the Sudan, which had claimed the attention and blood of British explorers, soldiers, and administrators for many years. Britain decided to return to the Nile.

For many years the Egyptian khedives had spent all

the income from their own country and had wasted huge sums borrowed from Europe. Under the wise control of Lord Cromer, Egypt had recovered from economic stagnation and the heavy burden of foreign debt.

In the front offices of government, Egypt was a sovereign state. In the back rooms the British "advisors" made the decisions.

The Egyptians had a new and efficient army. Britain controlled it. The new commander-in-chief was Sir Herbert Kitchener, who had been appointed over the heads of older, more experienced men. He had been active in Egyptian-Sudan affairs for a long time. He had fought and defeated the Dervishes as they moved toward the Egyptian border. He had guarded the border with well-trained Egyptian and Sudanese units.

Kitchener was, like Gordon, an army engineer. Unlike Gordon, he did his campaigning as an engineer. He was methodical; he gave himself to organization. He practiced economy of money, material, and men. The day of Gordon's use of irregulars was past. The reconquest of the Sudan required a cool, efficient planner. Kitchener was the man.

Britain had changed her plans but she had not changed her method. She "withdrew from active participation" in the new Sudan campaign. It was not easy for an observer to distinguish between active and inactive participation. Lord Cromer was in control in Cairo. Col. Kitchener was commander-in-chief of the Egyptian forces. But Egypt would be asked to pay the bills. Britain's "official" withdrawal from participation gave efficiency to the campaign. Cromer and Kitchener suffered little interference from London.

The new campaign would not consist of troops marching across the desert and others plowing the Nile in gunboats. The advance would have to be slow. Bases would have to be built. Each section of the country would have to be administered as it was retaken.

Kitchener's forces were already at Wadi Halfa, just inside the Sudan border. His lines of communication from Cairo were eight hundred miles long. And Omdurman, capital of the Dervish Empire, was still another eight hundred miles away.

He received his orders to advance in March 1896. The orders came from London. Troops, supplied by camel, went on ahead. The main task of his army was to construct a new railway that would bring the troops within striking distance of the Khalifa's capital.

By June of 1896 the northern area had been cleared of Mahdist forces. Their valor was undiminished but they were wiped out as they ran into the firepower of the re-equipped Egyptian troops.

With his northern forces defeated, the Khalifa did not again attempt a full-scale attack on the advancing army. His garrisons continued to harass the forces building the railway. He massed most of his army in Atbara and waited. The wait was long. The northern area had been taken by the Egyptian troops in six months. It would take another two years to bring them to the last battle against the Dervishes.

Kitchener's men destroyed one garrison after another as they moved southward. The battle of Atbara was one of the most vicious of the campaign. The Egyptian army, supported by British units, lost over five hundred men. But the opposing Dervish force of fifteen thousand was almost wiped out.

The Khalifa knew that the defeat of his forces at Atbara opened the way for the final drive on Omdurman. He rallied his men, preached to them, paraded them outside the city, and called all to the holy war against the invading infidel. He built forts and installations for the final defense of his territory.

Kitchener methodically built his railway, supplied his troops, and brought the surrounding country under his military administration. When the railway reached Atbara the final assault on Omdurman, sixty miles away, was prepared. From Atbara the troops would move by river and by desert track. Trains had brought enough supplies to Atbara to last the troops for three months. British units had reinforced the Egyptian army. Kitchener the organizer had left nothing to chance. Now his mettle as a front-line officer would be tested.

From the railhead the Anglo-Egyptian army moved southward, setting up camps, establishing a hospital under canvas, moving supplies forward. The building of the long line of communications, the smashing of the Dervish units along the way culminated in the Battle of Omdurman on September 2, 1898.

The Khalifa's army had not changed much from the days when, under the Mahdi, it swept all before it as it crossed and recrossed the Sudan's plains and deserts, finally destroying General Gordon and his men in Khartoum.

It was a different story with the Anglo-Egyptian troops. They had the latest weapons. They were well supplied by the railway and they had been trained to a high peak of readiness by their British officers.

The Khalifa must have known that he faced a new army. He may have thought that, as in the days of the

Mahdi, the intervention of Allah would make up the difference.

The force under Kitchener numbered about twenty-five thousand, about a third of which was British. The units were equipped with artillery pieces and machine guns. Kitchener's ten gunboats on the Nile carried thirty-six cannon and twenty-four machine guns.

The Khalifa had rallied sixty thousand men to meet the advancing enemy. By pre-Gordon standards, he had a force that from sheer weight of numbers, bravery, and fanaticism would be hard to defeat.

In the days of the Mahdi's unbroken victories, the Dervishes attacked, surrounded, and destroyed British and Egyptian units. Now the Khalifa and most of his army waited for the Anglo-Egyptian forces to approach.

The army from the north marched from the end of the railway in Atbara. The Khalifa's outposts were overrun one by one. Kitchener's men made their last camp only six miles from Omdurman.

The gunboats steamed up to the city and let loose with their guns. The walls of the city were breached, the Dervish guns were knocked out, and the defenders were driven from the river. This action was diversionary. The main force of the Khalifa was on the desert west and north of the city. Kitchener's long years of preparation and the Khalifa's long years of waiting were at an end.

Kitchener began the last stages of assault by sending messages to some of the Khalifa's emirs, suggesting that they try to convince their leader that resistance was futile. But this paper offensive failed.

The Anglo-Egyptian forces thought they knew what tactics the Dervishes would use against them. The Khalifa would be smart enough not to expose his army to the guns and rifles of the enemy. But the Khalifa did the unexpected. He moved out onto the desert before his capital city with all his massed forces.

In the intervening years the Dervish army had not changed much. The soldiers came marching toward the enemy, flags flying. They shouted and they sang. The combined sounds became a roar.

When the followers of the Khalifa came within reach of the Anglo-Egyptian guns and rifles, they did not falter. They fell by the hundreds to the merciless fire from the enemy.

But it was not all so easily ended. The Dervishes isolated one section of the Anglo-Egyptian forces and were about to wipe it out when help came. The Khalifa's forces were stopped before disaster befell the invaders.

Though the first Dervish units to meet the enemy were wiped out mercilessly, the rest of the force kept coming. They maneuvered themselves into position, isolated enemy units from each other, and came on with undiminished zeal and ferocity. At the peak of the battle, the decision could have gone either way. The British commanders made several errors on the field. The 21st Lancers, Winston Churchill among them, charged a small detachment which, when its men arose from their hiding in the low ravines, turned out to be a sizable force. The Lancers lost twenty-one men in the fight and their strength was further reduced by the loss of more than a hundred horses.

The Lancers were rescued. The charging Dervishes were decimated before they could be reinforced. The battle subsided. The Dervish army was broken.

If bravery, valor, and devotion to a cause won wars, the Khalifa and his men would have driven back the forces of the invader at Omdurman. The Anglo-Egyptian forces were not without bravery. But in the end, the war was won by well-trained troops under competent leadership and armed with the latest weapons.

The Mahdists in their final defeat lost over ten thousand in killed alone. Fifteen thousand or more were wounded. The forces under Kitchener lost forty-eight killed and three hundred and eighty-two wounded.

The Sudan would be back in the hands of the Anglo-Egyptian forces with the final capture of the Khalifa himself. This event was to be delayed, for the Khalifa and the emirs who remained escaped to the south. They made their way westward to their original haunts.

✕✕✕✕✕✕✕✕✕✕✕✕✕✕✕✕✕

7

The Condominium

✕✕✕✕✕✕✕✕✕✕✕✕✕✕✕✕✕

KITCHENER crossed the river to Khartoum. He went to the ruins of Gordon's palace in the midst of the decayed city, where he held a memorial service for Gordon.

Another half-ruin, the Mahdi's tomb, lay on the banks of the Nile in Omdurman. When Army engineers examined the remains and said the building was unsafe, Kitchener ordered it destroyed. If it were rebuilt, he reasoned, it might become the center of a revived Mahdism.

The Mahdi's bones were removed from the tomb and thrown into the river. The skull was retained and was later buried in the Northern city of Wadi Halfa.

With these duties completed, Kitchener surveyed the wreckage he had won. Thirteen years of Mahdist rule had left the country in ruins. The population was thought to have been reduced from eight to three million inhabitants.

Thousands of able-bodied men had given up their farms and their trades to serve in the Khalifa's army. Their wives and children had followed them. In the fighting with the Anglo-Egyptian forces, the loss of life had been heavy. The country needed peace and a return to work.

Egypt and Britain agreed to a joint administration of the recovered territory. The new creation was called "The Anglo-Egyptian Sudan." The chief executive was to be a British governor-general appointed by the khedive in Cairo subject to the approval of the British government.

First to be appointed governor-general of the Sudan was its conqueror, Sir Herbert Kitchener. He began an administration which would be more Anglo than Egyptian right down to the declaration of an independent Sudan in 1956.

The governors appointed to administer the provinces were not Egyptians. They were British Army officers. Their first duties were to maintain public security and to root out the last vestiges of the previous regime. They had to re-establish authority and justice and bring about a restoration of confidence. The Sudanese, weary of thirteen years of insecurity and anxiety, were ready for a return to quiet and peaceable living. Sudanese leadership was cultivated by the British authorities. The idea of "The Sudan for the Sudanese" began to form.

To train Sudanese for participation in the government of their own country, Kitchener established Gordon College. He appealed to his countrymen to provide funds for the building of this institution as a memorial to Britain's hero, Gordon of Khartoum. Kitchener asked for a hundred thousand pounds. The fund was oversubscribed by thirty thousand pounds. Gordon College became the one institution in which Sudan leaders were trained.

Elsewhere in Africa future political stability was to be complicated by the presence of large numbers of Asian merchants and British farmers. The British in the Sudan restricted the immigration of Asians and Europeans.

The British were able to establish their administration in the Northern, Arabic-speaking provinces without great difficulty. The South was a different matter. In that area there was nothing to build on.

To bring order out of chaos in the South, the new administration had to limit the number of Northern Sudanese allowed to live and work there. Years later when order was re-established, legitimate merchants were permitted to carry on their trade. Eventually Northern Sudanese traders, government officials, and employees were to be found in all important towns in the South.

British and Egyptian troops had moved southward into the Sudan by means of the railroad the army had built. With this line to start with, the Sudan Railways branched out to the Red Sea where a new city, Port Sudan, was built. Westward the line ran to El Obeid, the first large city to be overrun by the Mahdi's forces. A bridge across the Blue Nile at Khartoum permitted the railway to reach that city from the Egyptian border.

The British began work on an administration that would give the Sudan good government and would give the Sudanese a large place in the government of their own country. The Sudanese would face the demands of independence better equipped and trained than most of Africa's new nations.

The chief administrator under the governor-general

was the civil secretary. His department administered the country and controlled the police force, which was responsible for public security. Education was also the civil secretary's responsibility.

Schools were opened in the North by the government. In the South education was carried on by government through foreign mission societies.

In 1928 the government built a dam at Sennar on the Blue Nile, two hundred miles south of Khartoum. A corporation was set up to dig a network of canals and to irrigate a million acres of land for the production of long staple cotton. The government's share of the profits from the sale of cotton became its most important source of revenue.

British doctors took up their duties in the Sudan and organized the Sudan Medical Service. A few hospitals were built in the Northern cities and in the capital cities of the three Southern provinces. Dispensers were trained and were appointed to village clinics. In the South large populations were moved out of sleeping-sickness-infested areas. Later Sudanese doctors were trained.

The Sudan Veterinary Service was established. The diseases of camels were studied. Cattle plague and such diseases as bovine pleuropneumonia were studied and vaccines were developed to bring the diseases under control.

Sudanese were trained as stockmen. They learned to diagnose the diseases of animals. When a Department of Veterinary Medicine was established, Sudanese became full-fledged veterinarians.

The Department of Posts and Telegraphs pushed its lines into most of the inhabited areas of the country.

Postal services increased as demands increased. Most of the work in the department was carried on by Sudanese.

The Public Works department was responsible for the erecting of housing, public buildings, offices, and schools. Branches of the department operated in all the provincial capitals and in the larger towns. Sudanese artisans and engineers were trained to carry on much of the work of this department.

Far away in the bogs of the South and in the deserts and plains of the North, British officials with their Sudanese assistants were maintaining security and were building up necessary services. The British district commissioners were responsible to their provincial governors.

The district commissioners and their Sudanese assistants apprehended wrongdoers, presided over trials, gave sentence, and jailed those found guilty. There was little criticism of the justice they dispensed.

A battalion of British troops was always stationed in Khartoum. When the Royal Air Force became a part of Britain's military establishment, a unit of the service was stationed there also.

Apart from a short period when they were not permitted access to the Sudan, the Egyptian army also had a unit based in the capital city.

If Egypt had little part in the administration of the Condominium, she made up for it by her watch on the Nile. The River was Egypt's life. Without it there would be no Egypt.

The Egyptians built a dam at Jebel Aulia, thirty miles from Khartoum on the White Nile. The dam held back the waters until the gates were opened each year when the water was needed in Egypt.

The Nile is the most measured river in the world. To check its rise and fall Egyptians maintained a large establishment in the Sudan. A large dockyard near Khartoum serviced the steamers that plied the River. At Malakal, headquarters town of Upper Nile Province, the Egyptian Irrigation Service had a larger staff than that of the Sudan Government's administration of the entire province. Twice weekly launches stretched measuring cables across the Blue and White Niles from Uganda and Ethiopia to the Mediterranean. Every drop of rain was a statistic.

Under the condominium powers, the Sudan prospered. Every department necessary to effective government was set up. In those departments Sudanese began to move up.

8

The Missionaries

BEFORE the rise of the Mahdi, the Roman Catholics had made several attempts to open work in the Southern provinces and in the west. The priests in the South had been unable to make any impression on the tribespeople. The unsettled conditions made missionary work impossible. Catholic priests in the western Sudan had been taken captive by the Mahdi and had been held by the Dervishes for up to twelve years.

With the establishment of the Condominium, the Roman Catholics, most of whom were Italians, were permitted to return to the South.

The first Protestants to reach the Sudan were Anglicans and Presbyterians of the old United Presbyterian Church. When J. K. Giffen and Andrew Watson of the Presbyterian Mission and Llewellyn Gwynn and Mr. Harpur of the Anglican church reached Khartoum to discuss the opening of missionary work with the governor-general, the Khalifa was still at large. Not until he was finally defeated were missionaries permitted to travel to the South.

Kitchener hoped that the various denominations would get together to form a united church in the Sudan. It was soon evident that Anglicans and Presbyterians were too far apart to consider such a program. The Roman Catholics were even farther removed.

In order to prevent harmful rivalry between the missionary organizations, the administration resorted to a system of spheres. Each mission was given an area to which it was expected to confine its work. The Roman Catholics, Anglicans, and Presbyterians were given their spheres in the three Southern provinces.

A few years later the Sudan United Mission, Australian-New Zealand branch, entered the Sudan. Its work was started north of the Presbyterian stations among the Dinka on the White Nile. Later a work was commenced in the hills of Kordofan province among the Nuba people.

The Africa Inland Mission, which had been working in the Congo, Kenya, and Tanganyika for many years, opened a work in the far South of the Sudan, along the Uganda border, in the early nineteen fifties.

Missions were not permitted to carry on evangelistic work in the Northern provinces. The Anglicans, the Presbyterians, and the Roman Catholics opened schools and medical work in the North and the government opened its own schools there.

The missionaries in the South were confronted by a host of unwritten tribal languages. In the home countries little had been done to prepare missionaries in the field of descriptive linguistics. Some missionaries had a natural bent for this kind of work and they did well in reducing languages to writing and in preparing materials for the teaching of reading. Following the translation of reading material and the Scriptures, schools were opened on the stations. The response was poor. Parents saw no relation between schools and the herding of cattle and the growing of grain. They were beginning to recover from years of insecurity which had been caused by the activities of outsiders. Now schools were being promoted by a new though benign intruder. Sending their children to school did not contribute to the feeling of security the tribal people badly needed.

The healing of diseases was more readily understood by the tribespeople. Dr. Fraser of the Church Missionary Society began his medical work at Lui in the far South in the early days of the Condominium. The tribal people soon learned that they could trust the doctor's medicine. Later they believed him when he talked about the value of education. School work began.

Elsewhere the resistance to schools slowly broke down. Eventually each mission in the South had its central schools with "bush schools" scattered everywhere. The graduates of the station schools spoke English, not Arabic. They wore shirts and shorts, not the Arab dress. They were professing Christians, not Moslems.

The British could see that it would be beneficial to the tribespeople of the Sudan ultimately to be detached from the North and joined to the British colony of Uganda. The Southerners were never asked for their opinion on the subject. Few of them could have taken part in discussions. When Sudan affairs were discussed periodically only the Northern Sudanese, the Egyptians, and the British took part.

The British remained the special guardians of the Southern peoples. They also had responsibilities to promote the welfare of the whole Sudan. And Egypt expected her interests in the Sudan to be protected. Her soldiers and her money had played no small part in the reconquest of the country.

The elimination of Egypt by the British from full participation in the administration of the Sudan remained a live political issue in Cairo. Egyptian politicians believed that the people of the Sudan would gladly place themselves under the Egyptian crown were it not for British interference.

The Sudanese did not appreciate their exclusion from discussions that took place frequently between the British and the Egyptians concerning the Sudan.

In 1951, the Egyptians took matters into their own hands. Their Parliament enacted a bill which proclaimed Farouk "King of Egypt and the Sudan." A new constitution for the Sudan was announced. All of this changed nothing in the Sudan. Events within the country were of much greater significance.

Kitchener's Gordon Memorial College had been producing secondary school and college graduates since its opening in the early years of the century. After World War II these graduates began to demand the right to speak for all the peoples of the Sudan in negotiations about constitutional development in the country.

At the same time two Moslem religious leaders had emerged to make their views felt in political circles. The long-standing cleavage between pro- and anti-Egyptian Sudanese became a political reality. Following the defeat of the Mahdi's forces, it had been convenient for the

British to recognize and patronize the leader of the pro-Egyptian element.

As the tide turned, it became inexpedient for the British to support the Egyptian demands for sovereignty over the Sudan. The British turned cool toward the leader of the pro-Egyptian sect in the Sudan.

Waiting in the shadows was the posthumous son of the Mahdi, young Abdl Rahman el Mahdi. The British had given him a small pension and had removed him as a symbol of a revived Mahdism. The Mahdi's son was, for obvious reasons, opposed to any return of Egyptian rule over the Sudan. He was for eventual independence. The British "rehabilitated" him. The Sudan political parties were forming.

The Sudan was one of the first African countries to raise the cry for independence in the new post-World War II era. Britain did not try to stifle the demands; she tried to keep up with and channel them.

Before the war Britain took the first steps to bring the Sudanese into government consultations. Advisory councils were formed. These councils quickly led to the setting up of a legislative assembly. Northern Sudanese politicians built their political programs on the idea that there would be one united Sudan.

In 1947 the British authorities consulted Southern leaders on their political future. The Southerners, trusting British guarantees, agreed to become part of a united Sudan.

In 1948 elections to a Legislative Assembly were held. Local councils in the South chose thirteen representatives to the new body. The integration of South and North began.

For the first time the government opened its own schools in the South. In these Arabic was taught in addition to English and the tribal languages. Some missions introduced the teaching of Arabic into their schools. It was difficult for them to find non-Moslem Arabic teachers.

The few Southern Sudanese who had reached college level in the past had been sent to Makerere College in Uganda. Now they were to study at Gordon College in Khartoum. There, as in Uganda, they would study in English.

The setting up of a Legislative Assembly could not permanently satisfy the political aspirations of the Sudanese. The fact that they had two masters became a part of political reality in their country. The Egyptians debated the future of the Sudan in their parliament. The British negotiated directly with the Sudanese.

The overthrow of King Farouk and the establishment of a "democratic" movement in Egypt revived the hopes of the pro-Egyptian party in the Sudan. These same events strengthened the resolve of the leaders of the independence party to resist renewed Egyptian advances which, they knew, would be made even more attractive by the people who had gotten rid of the profligate Farouk.

The new regime in Egypt turned out to be more reasonable than its predecessor. With the exit of Farouk, Egyptian claims to sovereignty over the Sudan ended. The Egyptians agreed to recognize the right of the Sudanese to self-determination.

With Egypt now more co-operative, the move toward complete independence for the Sudan gathered momentum. Election machinery was set in motion. There was to be a house of representatives and a senate. The South, too, was to elect its members to Parliament.

When the results were counted, the pro-Egyptian party had won. Its leader, Ismael el Azhari, became the Sudan's first prime minister. But the British were still there. The Sudan now had self-government but not complete independence. Before this could come, there would have to be the election of a constituent assembly. This assembly would decide what form independence would take: union with Egypt, or complete independence from both Egypt and Britain.

But the Sudanese could not wait for cumbersome machinery to grind out independence. In December 1955, Azhari, the prime minister, presented a resolution to parliament. It said, "The Sudan has become a sovereign state." Without hesitation parliament approved the resolution.

January 1, 1956, was proclaimed as Independence Day. Invitations were sent to important persons to attend the celebrations. British and Egyptian officials were to do their part. The representatives arrived at the Houses of Parliament on the appointed day. They presented to the Sudan letters from their governments recognizing the independence of the new state. The prime minister, accompanied by his advisors and the representatives of the dying Condominium, proceeded to the palace grounds where the ceremonies were to be held.

For more than fifty years the flags of Egypt and Britain had flown side by side over all government headquarters throughout the country. In Khartoum they had flown on two staffs high over the palace in which General

Gordon had died. They were flying on that morning when the representatives of the Condomini arrived from the ceremony in the parliament buildings. Hundreds of guests filled the palace grounds.

Prime minister Azhari made a short speech. Then the British and Egyptian flags were slowly lowered for the last time while the Sudanese cheered wildly. The yellow, green and blue flag of the new Sudan was raised. The band played. Only three British officials were on hand for the last rites. The Sudanese began the huge task of governing their own sprawling country. The three British officials quietly withdrew, their work completed.

9

The New Day

A NEW DAY had dawned for the people of the Sudan. A new day had dawned also for the missionaries. The Sudan Interior Mission had entered the Sudan with the permission of British officials. Permits to enter assigned areas, to hold land, to erect buildings, and to carry on missionary work had been granted by them. We members of the Sudan Interior Mission had learned to live and to work in the colonial Sudan.

Not all our requests to the authorities for permits to enter new tribes and to initiate new types of work had been granted. Not all British officials believed in the value of missionary work. The British regime had passed. Would the new Sudanese government look upon us as a continuation of colonialism in their country?

As American and British missionaries in our organization, we believed that all people had the right to choose the type of government they wanted for their country. We did not begrudge the Sudanese their independence.

We rather gloried in it. We knew that our position in a predominantly Moslem state might be precarious. Still, we felt some of the exhilaration the Sudanese themselves felt.

In the past our official relations with the Sudanese had been mediated by the British. They spoke for the Sudanese in matters of government and education. Now we would be able to deal directly with the people of the country. The British had not allowed us to open work in the Ingessana tribe. We were optimistic enough to think that the Sudanese, desiring to be respectable among nations, might grant us the permission the British had denied.

The Sudan Interior Mission became a part of the Sudan scene in 1937 when missionaries, expelled from Ethiopia by Mussolini, began a work in that adjoining land. (When the Mission began work in Nigeria in 1893, the whole stretch of land south of the Sahara from Dakar to the Red Sea was called The Sudan. The French designated their part of this area as "The French Soudan." After World War II the various countries in this area became independent and took their own names or restored old ones. The name Sudan was left for the Republic on the Nile.)

My wife and I were among those expelled from Ethiopia. We had gone there in 1934 following our graduation from Wheaton College in Illinois, where we had met. I was a sophomore from Tacoma, Washington, when Enid Miller turned up on campus as a freshman from Milwaukee, Wisconsin.

Our college romance was strengthened by our mutual concern for Africa. Before we graduated, we applied to the Sudan Interior Mission, about which we knew very little, for service in Ethiopia, about which we knew even less. We were appointed to the work in the Eastern Fields of the Mission. The main body of missionaries were at work in Nigeria and its neighboring colonies in French West Africa.

The leaders of the Mission informed us that we would be expected to spend a year in Ethiopia, learning the language and getting into the work before getting married. By the time the year was up there were already rumblings of possible invasion of Ethiopia by the Italian Fascists.

We were married at our Soddu station in March 1935. We made our way with a string of pack mules and carriers to our assignment on the station at Bulki in Gofa Province, far from Addis Ababa and its new anxiety. Italy began its invasion of Haile Selassie's kingdom and eventually announced the complete conquest of the land. In a little more than three years from the time of our arrival in Ethiopia, we found ourselves in Addis Ababa on our way home. Mussolini had ordered the expulsion of all missionaries from his new colony.

In Addis Ababa we, with our fellow missionaries, surveyed the map of Africa. For some it was too late to make a change. They returned to their homelands. Others joined our Mission's work in Nigeria.

Those who had been successful in starting small churches in southern Ethiopia studied the map of the Anglo-Egyptian Sudan. Would it be possible to open new work in that land along the Ethiopian border and to keep in touch with the Christians who had been left?

The change from the cool highlands of Ethiopia to the hot plains of the Sudan would be hard to make. We had heard that British officials in the Sudan went home every year for three months. We could not afford that luxury.

We had studied Amharic, the national language of Ethiopia, and had dug out unwritten tribal languages. In the Sudan would we have to start again on tribal languages and perhaps learn Arabic?

In Ethiopia the government was in the hands of Orthodox (Coptic) Christians. In the Sudan Moslems were in the majority. How would we get along with them? Before taking up a new assignment in the Sudan, we returned to the United States to await the birth of our firstborn.

The S.I.M.'s first missionaries to the Sudan could not walk in and start work in an area of their own choosing. There would have to be consultations with the authorities and the granting of permits to build stations and to commence missionary work.

In order to negotiate with the British in the Sudan, our first workers took up residence in the City of Khartoum. They learned that all missions worked under the Director of Education. They called on him.

He was a kindly man and expressed sympathy for those who had been forced to abandon their young work in Ethiopia.

"In the South Sudan," he said, "the government does not do educational work. We give subsidies to the various missions and they operate the schools. If we agree to give you an area in which to work, you, too, will have to start schools. We will pay most of the cost of buildings, the boarding and clothing of the pupils, and we will also pay a grant to the missionaries who supervise the schools."

Our leaders went home to consider this arrangement.

Ethiopia had been easier. There missions had been given permission to open stations in certain areas. The languages of the tribes had been reduced to writing, clinics had been introduced, reading classes had been organized, the church had been established.

The policy of our Mission had been to bring people to the Lord through preaching and personal witness and to teach converts and their children in order to establish churches. Now we would have to reverse the order. Teaching would have to precede the organizing of the church.

"This is not the way to get the indigenous church established," our leaders said. "We will be tied to the classroom. There will be no time to preach. And the price is too high."

When the missionaries had concluded their discussions they decided the price was not too high. If they refused to pay the price, they would lose the opportunity of bringing the Gospel to hitherto unreached people of the Sudan.

The leaders returned to the Director of Education and told him of their decision. "We agree to start schools in the area you grant to us," they said.

Permission was requested to open work in the Ingessana tribe. We had learned that these people were attractive, industrious, and still unreached by any Christian workers. They lived not far from the Ethiopian border.

"We would like to begin our work in the Ingessana tribe," our leaders told the Director.

"I am sorry," he replied. "The Administration does not look with favor on your starting there. The Ingessana are isolated from other tribes and are surrounded by Moslems. The Administration does not wish to add to the difficulties of maintaining public security in the area by having a religious minority there."

Discussions and appeals followed but the answer was final. The Sudan Interior Mission could not enter the Ingessana tribe. The new work was commenced in the Maban and Uduk tribes farther south, with stations at Doro and Chali. These stations were fifteen to forty miles from the Ethiopian border and thirty miles apart. In December 1938 Enid and I returned from the United States and joined other missionaries at work on Chali station.

To the west of Doro the Maban tribe lived in scattered villages. Farther to the west there was an uninhabited plain. Then Dinka territory began and continued to the White Nile. The Sudan United Mission had been carrying on work among the Dinka for many years. Converts had been few. Farther west in the Nuba Mountains of Kordofan Province, the S.U.M. work had been more successful. Churches had been formed and there were numerous Christians.

The two missions discussed the future of the work in the Dinka tribe. The Sudan United Mission wanted to concentrate on its Nuba work so its leaders agreed to give us their Dinka stations.

By 1949 schools were in operation on three stations. It had taken a long time to gain acceptance for education among the tribespeople. The work was difficult. There were runaways and discipline cases. Parents took their children from school to take care of babies or to herd cattle or just to get them away from "the paper." Still, the Dinka, Maban, and Uduk people were hearing the Gospel and the children were learning.

10

※※※※※※※※※※※※※※※※※※※

Half a Loaf

※※※※※※※※※※※※※※※※※※※

IN 1941 Ethiopia was liberated from fascism by British and Belgian colonial troops and Ethiopian patriots. Our leaders, who began the work in the Sudan following the closing of our work in Ethiopia, now returned to their original assignments in Addis Ababa. Others followed in subsequent years. By 1947 all our original leaders had left the Sudan. That year I was asked to become field superintendent of our work.

We had been joined by several women at Chali. A boarding school was about to open. A clinic was treating hundreds of patients weekly. The church was beginning to grow. We turned the work over to these women and moved to Khartoum.

In 1948 the Ingessana people were still without a Christian testimony. So were the Gumuz along the Blue Nile on both sides of the Sudan-Ethiopian border. So were the Koma, Jum Jum, and Barun. Should we try to forget them or should we approach the authorities again for permission to open new work among these people? If anything was to be done, it was now my responsibility to do it.

We could not forget. I sent a letter to the authorities toward the end of 1948. "The Sudan Interior Mission herewith makes application to begin work in the Ingessana, Gumuz, Jum Jum, Barun, and Koma tribes," it said.

A reply came back promptly. "If your request is granted, you will not be required to do educational work. In the future the Department of Education will open its own schools. The Governor of the province and the District Commissioners concerned will have to be consulted," it read.

I would have to see these government officials before they made their decisions and sent their recommendations to the civil secretary, the chief administrator in Khartoum. I made an appointment with the governor of the Blue Nile Province. His office was in the Province Headquarters, a hundred miles to the south in Wad Medani.

The governor was friendly, relaxed, and willing to discuss our application. There were no other missions operating in the tribal area of his huge province. In Wad Medani the American Presbyterians and the Anglicans had work.

We looked at the floor-to-ceiling map on the wall of his office and I pointed out the sites we wanted to have for new mission stations. "Nobody else is doing anything for those people," he said. "I don't see why you shouldn't give them some help." I was encouraged.

"In any case I'll call my district commissioner up the

road and tell him what I think. When you get there he will be ready to discuss the matter with you," he continued.

The district commissioner was one hundred rough miles away. I got to his town and spent the night in the government resthouse. After breakfast I met him in his office. There were greetings and coffee. The discussions were not long delayed.

"As for the Ingessana, they are surrounded by Moslems. I want my district to progress socially, politically and economically. I will not agree to any element entering my area that might upset its progress."

I understood the English and the interpretation. The governor had looked with favor on our application. But even he would not want to remove this roadblock. Having the governor on our side would not be enough. But we were not through.

"As for Gumuz, Jum Jum, and Barun, I will recommend that you enter these tribes when you have developed fully your work at Chali and Doro," he ended with a full stop.

I wondered what he meant by "fully developed." The authorities in Khartoum would have to decide the meaning.

I did not accept the district commissioner's verdict. "According to our Christian faith, all men have the right to hear the Gospel. We cannot make them receive it but we should have the right to explain God's salvation to them," I said.

"If you make converts among the Ingessana," he replied, "they will be a minority in a Moslem area and that will add to our administrative difficulties. You will get into that tribe over my dead body," he said with finality. I knew I could make no further progress with him.

When I saw the governor again, he seemed somewhat embarrassed. "Apparently my commissioner doesn't think this is the time to open new work in his area," he said. "He does have a big job. He and his assistant administer an area as large as Palestine and I can sympathize with his wish not to have new work added to himself and his overworked staff. I can't very well override his wishes," he concluded rather sadly.

There was still the civil secretary in Khartoum, the Number One man in the government after the governor-general. I received an appointment to see him. I didn't want to wait until the letter came turning down our application.

"The governor seemed to think it would be good for us and good for the tribespeople to have work in the area I suggested to you," I said. "But the district commissioner was adamant in his objections. I trust, sir, that we will not be stopped by one man."

The civil secretary agreed to consider the opinions of all concerned. He would be writing me a letter.

When the letter came it brought us permission to open work in the smaller tribes; Koma, Barun, Jum Jum, and Gumuz. Again Ingessana was excluded.

The district commissioner was not happy that we had been given permission for this new work over his head. He quickly sent a new recommendation to Khartoum. "I suggest that the Sudan Interior Mission restrict themselves to the Koma, Jum Jum, and Barun tribes for the present. When the work in these places is well established, we can consider letting the Mission open work among the Gumuz people."

One man was concerned with the development of his district and did not want any new elements introduced. Perhaps he was thinking of promotion. It was too late for him, too. Independence would come first.

We had asked for a loaf of bread and had received half. Still the permission we did receive meant that hitherto unreached tribes would now be reached with the Gospel.

As for the two tribes that might never hear the message, a British official would have to answer for that. The Lord might send the Gospel to them some other way.

11

×※×※×※×※×※×※×※×※×※×※×

The "Irish Bridge"

×※×※×※×※×※×※×※×※×※×※×

THE LETTER from the civil secretary had said that we could open new work among the Koma, Jum Jum, and Hill Barun people. The name "Koma" was used to designate five tribes living along the Sudan-Ethiopian border south of the Yabus River and in both countries. It was due west of Addis Ababa. It was a sparsely settled corridor, twenty to thirty miles wide and a hundred miles long, untouched, unexploited, and only superficially explored. It was described by the London Institute of African Languages as a "linguistic no-man's land."

Sam Burns, a Britisher, and Chuck Guth, an American, were ready to open up the area. They were both single at the time. Chuck had matrimonial prospects, but Sam was unattached. They had been in the country for several months, had studied some Arabic, and were no longer strictly greenhorns.

Sam was not new to the Sudan. He had been attached to the Royal Army Medical Corps during the war and had been stationed in Khartoum for a while. He had attended meetings regularly at the Sudan Interior Mission headquarters and had heard much about the work in the South through missionaries who came and went. He had been demobbed after the war, had taken a course in linguistics at London University, and had returned to the Sudan as a member of the Mission.

Sam was English, Scots, or Irish depending on the person to whom he was speaking. His ancestry was Scottish but, with thousands of others, his people had gone to live in Northern Ireland and so Sam had grown up in Belfast. Then his people had moved to the Midlands of England and he had spent his late teen years there.

Some interdenominational and international missions, similar to the Sudan Interior Mission, give their American and British members separate areas in which to work. Perhaps it is necessary, in some cases, to avoid trouble by keeping nationalities apart, especially where the missionaries are "very British" or "very American."

Our Mission has often put individuals with a common origin on a station, New Zealanders together, Australians together, English together. But this is no guarantee that persons so placed will get along well. They still face the difficulties that arise from the fact that they are human beings.

Some "very British" and some "very American" missionaries have worked well together because they were genuine, gracious human beings.

Sam was of medium height, almost short. He was stocky and solid. His face revealed what was going on within. The serious mood of contemplation quickly gave way to a smile or a quizzical look that asked "What are you going to say now, something humorous or something serious for a change?"

The Plymouth Brethren had done a good job with Sam. He knew the Scriptures.

Chuck Guth had gotten his training at the Philadelphia College of the Bible and Wheaton College in Illinois. Spiritually and intellectually he was a sensitive young man. He was an artist but did not wear a turtle-neck sweater and a beret. Affectation was no part of him. He was as lean as a Sudanese during famine, prematurely bald and slightly stooped. This was not strange as he had hardly any middle to support him and his sensitive soul was easily weighed down with any lack of concord, any unhappiness, any hypocrisy he saw around him. And the burden in his soul showed in his heavily burdened shoulders.

He had faced the problem of a career. He loved to paint. It was as much a part of him as music was a part of Handel. Some persons are artists. Others merely paint. Chuck was an artist. We could expect this artist to be temperamental along with writers and musicians. But Chuck failed to be normal. He was as steady as a Sudan camel turning an oil press.

Young people with outstanding talents face the mission field with special concerns. How can they bury themselves in the bush, the village, or the jungle with the urge to write, to compose, to play, or to paint? These matters have to be taken into consideration. Then the final question has to be faced. "Lord, what wilt Thou have me to do?"

Chuck came to us with no regrets. But he had his paints, brushes, canvases, and palette with him. When anxieties mounted, work became pressing, or he felt the need to "get away from everything," he took his box down to the stream. He surveyed the river banks, the overhanging wild fig trees, a man perched on a stone (spear in hand ready to thrust at a passing fish), or a flock of inquisitive black-and-white Colobus monkeys resting in the lower branches of a tree. He chose a comfortable spot on a smooth patch of stone, spread his paints before him, and set to work. Soon he was lost in another world. When he returned to the real world, the anxieties and pressures were much easier to face. And another canvas was ready for use as a gift.

Missionary work makes strange partners. Chuck Guth from New Jersey and Sam Burns from Sutton Coldfield were to work together.

When permission came to open work among the Koma people, it was too late in the season to do any building. It was necessary to survey the area, to discover population centers, and to estimate the number of people living in the district. Water supplies had to be found. There was time for one survey trip before the rains set in. Sam and Chuck got their camping gear ready, bought food supplies, and we headed south. The Yabus River marks the northern boundary of the Koma people. To get there we had to travel five hundred miles from Khartoum in a pickup truck.

Early on the morning of the third day, we began to recognize the rocky hills and the scattered sycamore trees of the Yabus River plain. Six miles of cracked cotton soil separated us from the river.

The road was flanked by the charred desolation of a grass fire. Here and there clumps of grass had escaped

the flames. Twisted, dwarfed trees stood leafless and forlorn, feet in ash. The annual trial by fire was too much
for them. They would never grow tall.

Suddenly a lesser kudu, frightened by the noise of the
car, appeared through the scrub, leaped across the road
in front of us, head stretched forward in desperation,
twisted horns close to his neck. He disappeared in a
cloud of soot.

"Too bad we didn't get a shot," Sam said.

"I'd like him to pose in midair long enough for me
to paint him," Chuck added.

Each was speaking his own language.

The cotton soil had ended abruptly. The scrub had
given way to a line of spreading wild fig trees. They were
the sign that below a river flowed. We stopped suddenly.
Ahead of us and below us was the Yabus. The water we
saw had only recently left Ethiopia and had traveled
less than four miles in the Sudan. There was a considerable fall in the river at this point. The water, now at its
lowest level, babbled over the stones and solid rock
that formed the stream bed.

Most visitors to the river were mildly shocked when
they saw the bridge about which they had heard so
much. It was merely a slab of reinforced concrete. It was
out of water only when the river was low and was usable
for about six or seven months of the year. The rest of
the time it was impassable under two to fifteen feet of
water. We were told by our British friends that this kind
of construction was called an "Irish Bridge."

Uduk and Koma tribesmen were prowling in the water
among the stones in search of fish. Others were poised
on the banks, spear in hand. Still others were sitting

motionless, fishing with poles, string, and hook. We stopped the car. We looked down on the primeval, idyllic scene. If only our lives could be as restful! But were the fishermen below us at rest? They were fishing early in the morning because of anxiety. They knew what hunger was. If they caught no fish, many in the villages would go to sleep on empty stomachs that night.

These were the people Sam and Chuck would be reaching with the Gospel. For their sakes they would build their homes on this part of the earth's rim. The message they would introduce might some day help the people with their food supplies.

Chuck would bring his bride here. And Sam would do the same if the Lord should act to find one for him.

Sam had learned in the Brethren Assemblies that young men were not to court the ladies.

"When the time comes for you to marry," the leaders had said, "the Lord will show you the one He has chosen for you."

Sam was well into his thirties and the Lord hadn't given him any revelation yet. Could it be that the Lord expected him to take some initiative, Assemblies' doctrine notwithstanding?

Sam was having serious theological doubts. But he would have to get through the next two years of building, language research, and anthropological study. Then, perhaps, he could review his theology of courtship and do some investigating.

Before the end of the two-year period he concluded that the Brethren were right. The Lord was in the delay. He brought the right girl into Sam's life.

12

Along the Border

✳✳✳✳✳✳✳✳✳✳✳✳✳✳✳✳✳✳

ACROSS THE GORGE and at about our level stood several native-style bamboo-walled grass-roofed buildings. Government officials and visitors trekked to this point when they wanted a few days' fishing or hunting. Waterbuck, hartebeeste, roan antelope, and the beautiful, ubiquitous oribi could be shot with a little effort. Chief object of hunters was the lion. This animal prowled around the villages, looking for goats and sheep when wild game was scarce. Lions were most plentiful in the rainy season when the roads were closed to hunters from Khartoum. There were no cows along the Yabus. This was tsetse fly country. Fortunately the type of fly present confined its activities to animals. Men were not infected by its bite.

We rolled down the hill to the bridge and roared up the opposite bank. A small detachment of mobile police was in residence. The men lolled in the shade of the myrrh-bearing shrubs. Their mules munched green grass that had been brought from the river.

"*Salaam alekum*," we greeted the corporal as we stepped down from the truck.

"*Alekum es Salaam*," he replied and his four men joined in the greetings.

Arabic was not their mother tongue and it certainly was not ours. They spoke three different languages among them: Dinka, Moru, and Bari. All were from the far South Sudan. They talked to each other in Arabic of sorts. Our conversation with them had to be in this language.

"We are going to Dajo to see the people and the country," I said.

"You are going to have a mission there, we heard," the corporal replied. "It is good. Nobody is helping these people. They don't even wear clothes. What kind of people are these?"

The police we met were Southerners. They had been to mission or church schools. They had learned to read and had had a little instruction in numbers, geography, drawing, and the Scriptures. They had learned enough to know they didn't want to return to backbreaking farm work again. They had wandered away from home, and had joined the police force.

The corporal and his men went back to their shade and we took the road toward the south. Here the trees had succeeded in getting ahead of the fires. They were tall and gaunt. They had shed their leaves in the rainless winter and the fires had leaped up to devour any that remained.

The flora changed with the soil. We had gone through

the scrub-bearing cotton soil. It produced heavy crops of grass, allowing the fires to burn fiercely and to destroy all the trees. Now we were traveling on red, gravelly soil. It was not as rich as the cotton soil so it did not produce a heavy crop of grass to serve as kindling to the trees.

The Komas had done a good job of clearing the grass from the road. This "forced labor" was part of their tax payment. In addition they paid forty cents per year in cash. They had filled the big holes with dirt and grass. Still, the road was not smooth.

There were no bridges across the stream beds. All were dry now. The banks, which were washed away each year, had been cut back, allowing a vehicle to roll down to the bottom and roar up the other side. In some places the sand had been covered with dirt to give traction to the wheels. We couldn't expect more. Only half a dozen cars and trucks passed this way each year.

All three of us had become bird watchers. Our text had been *A First Guide to South African Birds*. It was a pleasant hobby, especially on such trips as we were making. It helped to while away the hours and took no time from more useful pursuits when we were on our stations.

"Do you see those two ground hornbills through there?" Sam asked, pointing to the right.

There they were, their feathers shiny black, their heavy turned-down beaks covered by a small, turkey-like red comb. They held their heads erect and stood looking at us. We were getting too close. They flapped their heavy wings, bounced along the ground for a few feet, then climbed heavily through the trees.

Graybilled hornbills screeched as their larger relatives

invaded their treetop territory. The graybills dropped out of the trees, spread their wings, and flew away, their up-down, up-down flight identifying them as much as their beaks. On the last swoop upward, they dropped their feet and lit on branches out of reach of our noisy contraption.

We were averaging fifteen miles an hour. Our average would be lowered during the next two hours. We would have to climb the mountain, which now loomed before us. It rose two thousand feet above the plain on which we were traveling. I speeded up the engine and hit the first rise hard. It was the only way to climb with a three-speed transmission. It was hard on the truck. The tires hit the stones, and the rear wheels spun in the loose gravel, but we made it.

We circled around the side of the next protruding hill, turned toward the mountain, and roared up the next steep mountainside. We were getting high enough now to enjoy the view below. Finally we reached the top. The ridge top was about six feet wider than the car. We looked down the slope two thousand feet on either side. The air was heavy with smoke and unwashed dry season dust brought by the khamseen, the fifty days' north wind, and left suspended in the air awaiting the air conditioning the rainy season would bring.

To the east the ground dropped away from us to the valley floor and then began the ascent to the mountains of Ethiopia. We could see them dimly outlined through the haze. There were Koma people living up there. But somewhere between us and them there was an imaginary line, an international boundary. To visit that part of the tribe we would have to have entry permits. But to whom would we show our passports when we crossed the unmarked border? We would someday see.

The heat of the plain we had just left arose like the smoke from Sodom and Gomorrah.

"It's too bad we can't live up here instead of down in that furnace," Chuck mused thoughtfully.

As we descended from the mountaintop, the engine got a rest while the brakes took over. There were still thirty miles of cracked cotton soil to travel before we would reach the Dajo River and resthouse. We would find a permanent police post and small settlement there. The early rains had carried away one of the two bridges in the Dajo area. But we managed to throw enough logs and dirt into the roadbed to make the crossing.

"It's beautiful country around here," Chuck said, his arm describing the nearby Ethiopian foothills and valleys. "Look at that river. You can't see it but you can tell by the line of green trees where it is. And the bamboo forests go right up to the tops of the mountains. Man, that's beautiful!"

We drove up to the police post. There were numerous mud and thatch buildings forming a compound. This was the police headquarters. Nearby was a resthouse and a lonely Arab traders' shop. All the roofs had been thatched with coarse grass, which had been laid in steps. There were palm trees scattered through the village. It looked like a scene from the travels of David Livingstone. Perhaps our own feelings affected what we saw. We were far away in the middle of a never-never land.

Twice a year the British district commissioner from Nasir, to the south on the Sobat River, visited Dajo, accompanied by sixty Nuers carrying his personal belongings, his food, and his whiskey. Between the two visits the police and the Koma got on as best they could.

The corporal of police welcomed us as his men gathered around. A few nondescript Komas stood just outside the circle. They never felt that they "belonged" even in their own country. Their fathers and mothers had learned to bend low to outsiders. The presence of the police with their forced labor served to keep the Komas "down" where they themselves seemed to think they belonged. Whenever a Koma or Uduk met an Arab or a Southern policeman he took his place . . . down low.

We unloaded the goods that would keep Sam and Chuck comfortable and fed for six weeks. They had their notebooks and would chart all the villages within a radius of thirty miles. They would make a census. We would then know how to plan the work for the Dajo end of the tribe.

Our sandwiches and tea were finished. I needed to hurry to get back to Chali before bedtime. "I'll try to be in the Doro area in about six weeks," I said cheerfully. Sam and Chuck would have to walk one hundred and fifteen miles to meet me.

"I don't know how long it will take us to get there but look for us about April 15." Sam was turning the pages of his pocket diary.

I felt like a deserter leaving them, knowing that the rains would come, the streams would wash out the roads, and I would be unable to return to Dajo to help them. I would spend the intervening time in the comfort of Khartoum.

We prayed together, asking the Lord to guide us in

this important task of finding the right place from which to reach the mixed-up Koma tribes. We knew that at best Dajo would have to be a dry season center from which the surrounding villages could be reached. Because of its isolation the government would not let us station missionaries there during the rainy season.

I left Sam and Chuck and turned northward. I knew that this Anglo-American team would have a first-class report of the area and its people at the end of their six-week stay. They were that kind of men.

I stopped on the mountaintop to look across the valleys again. The sun was low at my back as I looked up to the Ethiopian mountains to the east. The last rays of light cut through the haze and turned the hills to gold in one last burst of splendor before darkness fell. I reluctantly returned to the truck and started down the mountainside into the hot, flat plain.

13

※※※※※※※※※※※※※※※※※※

A Broken People

※※※※※※※※※※※※※※※※※※

SIX WEEKS later I drove south from Khartoum and met Sam and Chuck on schedule at Doro.

"It's a good thing we didn't wait for you at Dajo," Sam sighed. "The streams are all flowing from the Ethiopian mountains and it would have been impossible for you to get through. The road is washed out at every stream." And there were dozens of them.

"Oh, man. I don't know how I ever made it," was all Chuck had to say.

A man in good condition should be able to walk twenty-five miles a day for several days in a row in a temperate climate. But when the temperature is 100 degrees, the road is a foot-wide path frequently flanked by thorns, and covered with slimy mud, it is more like traveling fifty miles each day.

Back in Khartoum Sam and Chuck settled down to Arabic study. They were both good students. They helped in the services we held twice each Sunday and in the classes we held to teach English to Sudanese, most of whom were Moslems.

The Sam-Chuck partnership was going to have to undergo a change. Betty Bear and Chuck had "an understanding." Soon after Betty's arrival from America the understanding gave way to an engagement.

The rains were coming to an end down south and we were anxious to return to Koma country to pick out a site for the station. We would have to find it, measure it, make a drawing of it, submit the plan to the provincial authorities, and then wait for a reply before doing any actual building.

The rains show signs of ending early in October in the southern tip of Blue Nile Province. But it takes another six weeks and more before the roads are dry enough to allow travel by car. It was the last week in November when we headed south again in the new pickup truck of which Chuck had taken delivery during the rains.

We had no trouble until we reached the Yabus River. We stopped at the top of the bank and stared down at a roaring torrent. We had never before seen it at this stage. Much of the "bridge" was invisible beneath the roaring water.

We left the truck and walked down to the water's edge. Some Komas on the opposite side came across to us. They moved cautiously on the slime-covered cement. The water was only fourteen inches deep on the bridge but it was running fast. With the help of the Komas we stretched a rope along the upper side of the bridge. We took off our shoes and socks and waded across, hanging on tightly. It was hard to keep our footing. Then the great debate began.

"What do you think, Chuck? It's your truck."

"What do you think, Mal? You've been around longer than we have."

"What do you think, Sam? Can we make it?"

We discussed water pressures, the possibility of the water piling up against the truck and pushing it over the side, or the danger of the engine getting wet and stalling in the middle of the stream. Should we go slow or should we hit it hard?

We would probably roar across in thirty seconds and wonder why we had been so anxious. I got into the cab, drove down to the water's edge, had another look at the rushing water, and then hit hard. The water splashed over the hood. It piled up against the side of the car. But before anything could go wrong, the front wheels were on dry ground. The engine stalled. But it didn't matter. Sam and Chuck walked across, hanging on to the rope. We looked at each other as if to say, "How does one know whether to be careful or impetuous?" We had been stuck in the mud often enough to know that a little impetuosity can result in long delays.

In a few minutes the water had evaporated from the hot engine and we drove on. We wanted to visit the string of villages at Yeshkap, thirty miles south of Yabus. We were soon there.

Koma villages seem as forlorn as ghost towns. We want to say "Where is everybody?" but everybody is right there. The people are quiet. There is little activity in their villages. There are no markets. The huts are scattered, three here, two half a mile away. Each house is surrounded in the rainy season by a garden, about as large as a Philadelphia front lawn. A few miles away the residents cultivate their crops of sorghum. The total food supply is not sufficient to feed the village mouths. The men fish during low river and dry their catch for use in the rainy months. They dig rats out of their burrows and dig honey out of the trees, assisted in their search by the honey guide, a bird that leads men and beasts to hives in hollow trees and which feast on the honey the robbers leave.

Nowhere have we felt pity for people as for the Koma. They have very little present, hardly any future, and there seems to have been no past, certainly no past that one wishes to remember. Slave raiding, intertribal warfare, and insecurity prevailed for the Komas long after peace had come to Central Africa. The endless struggle to keep alive had given them their character. They had long since lost incentive. In recent years they had enjoyed the security the government had brought them. Yet the events that preceded the advent of security still governed their lives. Why plant a large crop when others would get most of it? Why protect the children? Let them be taken so that we can live in peace. Why build a good house? The termites will destroy it as quickly as a poor one. Why keep chickens, goats, and sheep? Others will enjoy them. They were a broken people.

Could they be rehabilitated, re-educated? Could a new spirit be given to them? The British government had done very little for them apart from giving them public security. The merchants had done nothing. The Komas had done little to improve themselves. We believed that the Gospel of the grace of God received by these tribespeople could do more than anything else to lift them out of their defeat.

Morning and evening we prayed together. "Lord, help us to help these Komas. Lord, they are so scattered, so divided by language. Show us where to live while we reach them."

The Dajo area was the most heavily populated. But with restrictions on us because of its isolation, we would have to choose Yeshkap or the Yabus River itself. A native-style house would have to be built at Dajo. The missionaries could take turns staying there for a few weeks at a time while trying to establish a solid work. A few days' preaching here and a few days' visiting somewhere else would not likely produce permanent results in the form of a church. And how much time did we have left to carry out our program for the Komas? We did not know.

We returned to the beautiful Yabus River. We left the truck at the resthouse and walked upstream through grass, brush, and creepers. About half a mile from the resthouse we came to a slight rise. It was not a level piece of ground. But each high spot would be large enough to hold a building. There would be no water problems. The Yabus, one of the few perennial streams in hundreds of square miles, gurgled past the site all through the dry season. During the rains it roared past like a subway train.

The tall trees away from the river were bare, the ground strewn with leaves and dry grass. The river bank itself was covered with green vines. Tall sycamore trees, their roots partly exposed by the river, leaned out over the water. A fish eagle called forlornly from atop a snag upstream. High overhead a lonely bataleur eagle let out its plaintive call. A troop of grivet monkeys chattered as they pounced from limb to limb, tree to tree. They, too, were investigating.

We noted the spot well. Then we walked upstream. There were Komas following us now. Life had been cruel. There wasn't much left for them. Could these "Turuks"— they knew no other name for us—possibly do anything to help them? We went on. Some otherwise promising spots were full of holes left by Koma and Berta gold diggers. They made a little money on the side digging and panning. They spoiled the ground wherever they dug. We were getting too far from the villages. We returned to the place of the fish eagle and the monkeys.

I didn't want to say, "This looks like the place," and discourage Sam and Chuck from making suggestions. All I said was, "This is a pretty good site."

"Yes," Sam joined in, "we could really do something with this spot."

Chuck wasn't worrying about swaying us one way or the other. "Imagine living in a beautiful place like this!" he exclaimed. "How about building our house on that rocky outcrop just back from the river?"

Our discussion was moving along rather rapidly, passing by some important considerations. "You'll be getting married one of these days, Chuck. After that, how are you going to keep the children out of the river?"

"That's a beautiful site for a house. Look, the foundation is already laid. That's almost solid rock. I guess we can keep the kids out of the water. I really don't know much about that yet." Chuck was ready to lay bricks.

I had to go more slowly. I had been on mission stations where present staff found it difficult to understand why the station hadn't been placed on a much better site not far away. I didn't want to have to live with regrets. I could see that I was being influenced by Chuck's enthusiasm. Sam was ahead of me, just behind Chuck and catching up rapidly.

14

※※※※※※※※※※※※※※※※※※※

No Passports

※※※※※※※※※※※※※※※※※※※

WE HAD ONE MORE QUESTION to answer
before settling down to the task of choosing a station site.
We had not visited the Koma people to the east. We had
heard descriptions of the villages up that way but we
needed to learn something about them for ourselves. We
knew that a "very big village" could consist of ten huts
and "many, many people" might mean fifty or sixty.
Sudan government figures gave the number of Komas as
three to four thousand. We suspected that there might
be a similar number across the border in Ethiopia. If
the Sudan Komas were living in defeat and hopelessness,
it was quite possible that those across the border were
even more desolate in their isolation.

The Sudan-Ethiopian border was just four miles from
the site we were eying. We wanted to visit the Komas
across the border but we didn't want to create an international incident. If our presence in Ethiopia were known,
somebody would be sure to say that "American and

British spies had crossed the border in search of buried Italian gold."

We had no evil intentions. We merely wanted to locate the last unvisited pocket of Koma villages. It was very unlikely that we would see anybody across the border who had heard the words "visa" and "passport."

There would be no motor road to follow. There would be game trails undistinguishable from Koma paths. We would be in an uncharted wilderness and it would be folly for us to be alone. Some of the local Komas agreed to accompany us.

The next morning we started out before the sun was above the horizon. We envied our Koma companions when it came to travel. Each man picked up his spear and throwing stick and started walking. Our equipment was simple enough. We had blankets and mosquito nets tied in rolls around our shoulders. The Komas carried our small bag of sandwiches and canned food.

Each of us carried a canteen of water. In my pocket I had a bottle of chlorine pills to use in the water we would pour into the canteens along the way. Somewhere we had packed two knives and some matches. A Boy Scout might have been horrified at our lack of preparation for so strenuous a journey.

We were in high spirits as we hiked along at a good pace. It was relatively cool. The temperature hadn't started up from its night-time low of 70°. The black drongo seemed to be sitting on every tree watching our muleless caravan.

We soon left the forests of the Yabus and came out onto a little plain. There were a few small villages here and there. We asked the people whether they were Sudanese or Ethiopians.

"We belong to the government," they said. They were Sudanese. They had never heard of the Sudan nor had they heard of Ethiopia. The *hakuma* (the government) meant the few British district commissioners they occasionally saw at the Yabus Bridge. The Ethiopians were "Habesh, Galla, Kujul." In fact the Koma people had never heard of Africa.

"Let's have a look at your map," I said to Sam.

He pulled it out of his pack and we spread it on our hands. We could see the two hills that marked the boundary at that point. We drew an imaginary line between the hills. It was back of us. We were in Ethiopia. There was no rope stretched along the border, there were no piles of stone to indicate its location. Like crossing the equator, there was nothing to see.

"Where is the border between the two countries?" we asked the villagers.

They pointed ahead to a line of trees along a rainy season stream bed. "Beyond that stream it is the land of the Gallas," they said.

We sat down and asked questions of the people. Where were the other villages? How many chiefs were there? How far was it to the villages on the side of Banga Mountain?

"There are not many villages," they said. "The chief is at Banga but it is very far away. We don't drink beer there."

We had learned that a village was not more than three hours' walk away if the people said "We drink beer there." It was one of the local measurements of distance. If they didn't drink beer at Banga, it would be far away. We knew it must be far away for another reason. Africans know that travelers, their own people or foreigners, want to be told that their objective is near. So, wanting to please, they usually say that the place in question is "very near." These people said it was "very far." It must have been true.

We explained our mission in Koma country. We told them about God, about His son, about salvation. We spoke in primitive Arabic. It was hard for us to explain our message. It was even harder for them to understand. Their limited knowledge of Arabic did not make it possible for them to understand the talk of God. Perhaps soon they would hear the talk in their own language.

We started on our way again. The sun was no longer cool. We began to sweat and we would keep on sweating until after sunset. We would have to climb for hours before reaching Banga. Ahead of us lay a once-beautiful bamboo jungle. Its straight stalks and feathery leaves were now brown and gray as it spread out through the valleys and over the hills. We asked the Komas what happened.

"The bamboo is dead," they said.

I had seen this before in the far South Sudan. At that time an official in the Sudan Forestry Department had explained that the bamboo goes to seed every twenty-two years. It blossoms, produces a cocklelike seed, and then the stalk dies. Whole bamboo forests go through this dying stage at once. Then a few miles away new forests spring up from the scattered seed.

Before us lay unknown square miles of dead bamboo. The stalks had fallen like matchwood across the road. We climbed on top of the crisscross sticks and made our way painfully and slowly, like men crossing on the beams of an unfinished house. A beautiful stream, a branch of the Yabus, gurgled by below. It had no trouble getting through the tumbled-down bamboo.

We were about to give up when suddenly, the path was clear again. It was noon and hot and we were about to leave the stream but first we would eat, swim, and rest. The Komas suggested that crocodiles were occasionally seen at this point. Chuck and I appreciated the warning but Sam insisted on getting cool. He took a couple of quick passes at the water, then dressed again.

The afternoon was waning when we came to the foot of a sharp peak, several hundred feet high. We were certain the path would circle it. But, no, it went right up to the top. As we climbed, our muscles grew tight and painful. Every movement required a lash of the will. Coordination was at a minimum. Our legs seemed to dangle. Drinking from our canteens was not a very satisfying experience. As soon as the water was swallowed, there was a strong urge to drink again. Our mouths were permanently dry and rigid.

We made it to the top of the hill and had no trouble getting down the other side. Then the road leveled off. The country ahead began to look inhabited. There was about an hour of daylight left when we saw the first huts. We were far from London and New York; far from Khartoum and far from Chali and Doro. And we were far from Yabus Bridge. Time had left us. Eternity had begun.

We dragged into the village. All was quiet. The dogs barked briefly and walked away. The men were back from their day's foraging for honey and for wild, edible fruit and roots. They looked dull and weary. It seemed that they had just come into the world and were waiting for the happy day when they could leave it again. There seemed to be nothing to detain them here for long.

The chief appeared and we chatted with him. He had traveled beyond his own area and knew that there were at least some people in the world beside the Komas.

"If you will give these men something to eat, we will pay you," I said.

"We have nothing to eat," the chief replied. "See the women are sitting. There is no grain for them to grind."

"These people really are poor," Chuck exclaimed. "I don't see any sheep or goats or anything."

"Don't you have sheep and goats here?" Sam asked the chief.

"We don't have anything," the chief replied with bitterness. "They took our animals long ago. When they come now they take our grain. And we have to pay them money for taxes. They give us a little piece of paper for this."

It was the sad plight of the exploited tribespeople in loosely administered, isolated areas. Tax collectors and administrators made the most of it. And if they left the people to starve and the babes to cry night after night in hunger, who cared?

The tender mercies of the heathen are cruel. Where Christian influence has not penetrated there is no feeling, no pity. There is similar exploitation and lack of compassion in the wilderness areas of New York, Chicago, London, and Paris. But the Komas here seemed so alone. There was no prospect of any relief. They would die and nobody would hear the death wail. Nobody would care.

We hacked down some tall grass in a nearby field and made beds for ourselves. We used bamboo canes to support our mosquito nets. We stretched our blankets over the grass. Our beds were ready.

It was dark. The people lit a fire. Nobody could deprive them of this amenity as long as trees grew. We were a miserable lot seated in the flickering light. When we assumed our positions on the ground, we could hardly move. Our legs were solid iron. Our guides were deeply engrossed in conversation with the local villagers. Their tones were low and earnest.

We carried on our conversation with the chief. His Arabic was almost as good as ours. We told the chief what had happened in our country. Our people, too, had been poor, defeated sinners. But God had saved us. It would take more than one evening to explain this to him.

We had come to find out about the people. "Are you as many as the Koma people in the Sudan?" we asked.

"As many," he replied. "Our villages follow your villages from the Yabus River to the Dajo. In some places we drink beer together."

Even if the authorities in the Sudan permitted us to build our Koma station at any place of our choosing, it would be difficult to pick a site from which we could reach all the people. We would have to build a station. When the people in the vicinity of our mission center responded to the preaching and teaching of the Word, they would have to carry the message to the people hidden in the villages of this border country.

We slept well. There was nothing else to do. When we awoke, there was a faint light over the mountains to the east. Africa's most familiar early morning sound was missing. We heard no roosters crow. There were none. We stood up. We rolled up our nets and blankets. We had a time of thoughtful prayer together. Then we said our farewells.

We walked along quietly, meditating. There is nothing more disturbing than to see hunger and sorrow and to know nothing can be done about it. International boundaries, protocol, and self-consciousness in high places would make a protest difficult and certainly inadvisable.

Our guides "knew another way" back to the Bridge. It was 25 per cent shorter than the route of the previous day. Why they hadn't brought us on this path we did not know. It did not climb hills and it did not go through the bamboo tangle. Nor was it as beautiful as the one that went through yesterday's forests. Our legs were like stilts for the first hour but limbered up with the forced walking. We returned to the one job left to us.

Once again we paced across the site. We marked off the boundaries of the proposed station. We picked sites for future buildings and looked over garden spots.

"How are we going to get in and out of this place and how are we going to send and receive mail when the river is high?" Chuck asked.

"We'll stretch a cable across the river" I suggested, "and you can ride in a little basket suspended under it." We all laughed.

We had chosen the site. Now there would be a mad rush to get government permits and to build a house before the rains again brought travel and building work to a stop.

The governor would have to approve of our choice of

a site. We would have to measure the boundaries accurately, show their relation to the compass, and describe the angles. The site plan would have to go to the survey department in Khartoum for approval. A formal lease would have to be drawn up by the legal department. I would have to sign the lease after producing my power-of-attorney.

Bricks would have to be made and burned on the spot. Lumber for the roof and for doors, windows, and frames would have to be shipped from Khartoum along with hardware. Some lumber could be cut from the surrounding forests. And somewhere between the bricks, nails, and doorknobs, Chuck and Betty would have to be married.

I left Sam and Chuck to start the waiting process. They would have to build a hut, explore their five acres further, make friends with the people around them, and begin to dig out the unwritten Koma language. I would have to get tentative permission for them to occupy the site.

The dry season was half gone when we received permission to build the Yabus station. Chuck and Sam hired Arab masons, burned bricks, dug foundations, and built a house. It took long hours of work and anxiety to build a comfortable bungalow in such an isolated place. There were months of manufacturing materials from dirt and trees and hours of bickering with skilled and unskilled workmen. Without the help of trade unions they were expert in the art of putting pressure on the manager at the right time and place to get higher wages and "fringe benefits." The latter included a longer breakfast hour, free sleeping mats and blankets, the supply of empty gasoline cans, and the right to draw on the unearned wages.

In the midst of the hard work Chuck returned to Khartoum. He and Betty were married in the Anglican Cathedral of All Saints by the Right Reverend Maurice Gelsthorpe, Bishop in the Sudan. The friendly, humble Bishop used a modified Anglican service. I gave the bride away.

Mr. and Mrs. Charles Guth established their first home in the new brick house on the banks of the Yabus River. Sam built a mud-brick hut a hundred yards away. He was taken in as a boarder by the newlyweds. He had no housekeeping facilities of his own. Life on African mission stations often begins this way.

There was still the problem of crossing the river during the six months of high water. The idea of a cable car was no joke. "Dear Sam," I wrote from Khartoum. "You had better find a site for a cable car and send me the measurements from tree to tree. I can get the cable from one of the iron workers here and he can make the car."

Sam sent the measurements by return mail. The Greek iron fabricator caught on to the idea quickly. He had the half-inch cable to support the "car" and a smaller size to wind the "car" back and forth. I showed him our design. Me made it according to our drawings and specifications. The metal basket, shaped like a bassinet, could hold two persons or one person and his personal effects for the road. Two pulleys were set in the overhead straps that came up from the "car." Near each tree there was to be a pulley for the winding cable to pass through.

On the station side there was to be a drum and a handle. The cable would pass around the drum, winding the car either across or back.

Large cable, small cable, cable car, crank, and pulleys were all sent south on a merchant's truck. Several weeks passed before I heard about the installation.

"It works," Sam wrote. "We have all tried it. This is really the answer. It will help to relieve the anxiety of our isolation."

15

❋❋❋❋❋❋❋❋❋❋❋❋❋❋❋❋❋❋

Last Station

❋❋❋❋❋❋❋❋❋❋❋❋❋❋❋❋❋❋

YABUS BRIDGE had been added to the list of Sudan Interior Mission stations. Sam Burns and the Guths were hard at work digging out the Koma language. All had had linguistic training.

The rains would be over again and we would have to prepare for the opening of work in the Jum Jum and Barun tribes. These people were not as isolated as the Koma and we knew the inhabited areas and centers of population.

Government officials did not want us to locate the Barun station near the Moslem town of Kurmuk. We didn't see much reason for this attitude, as our missionaries had had to use Kurmuk as their base for supplies and communication for years. Relations with Sudanese government officials and traders had always been good. We didn't think our presence five miles away would cause any anti-Christian feeling.

But the official who "wouldn't let us in except over his

dead body," was still in charge of the area so we had to choose a station site some twenty miles from Kurmuk.

We found a permanent water supply in the form of a rainy season stream which flowed past a suitable site for a Barun station and then went past the edge of the Jum Jum tribe, providing water for a station there. During the dry season, water could be pumped or dipped from holes in the sand which covered the bed of the stream to a depth of three to ten feet for miles.

The country was gently rolling, the surface of the ground broken by watercourses which carried water only during the rainy season. Back from the Maiak stream, a rocky hill rose sharply to a height of five hundred feet above the plain. In the distance to the east the mountains of Ethiopia stood up from the plain, looking unreal in the haze.

The Yabus scene was re-enacted at Maiak and Wadega. But there were variations. At Yabus we had not been required to get the permission of the local chief to choose a site, since it was in Upper Nile Province, one of the predominantly non-Moslem provinces. Maiak and Wadega were in Moslem Blue Nile Province, the northern boundary of which was only thirty miles from Khartoum. Non-Moslem tribes lived in the southern tip where it meets the Upper Nile. We were told we must get the permission of the two chiefs concerned before deciding on the sites we wanted.

The Wadega chief readily agreed to our choice of a site. At Maiak it was a different matter. The chief claimed to be one of the old Fung rulers. His people who once ruled the entire area as far as Khartoum were now farmers and minor chiefs and many had only a much diluted form of Islam. But their loyalties were in that direction. The local chief was, to all appearances, a Barun. But he wanted us to believe that he was superior to the people he ruled.

Mr. and Mrs. Joe Nash were to open the station. Joe and I were camped in the open air on the site we had chosen. We invited the chief to see the place and to visit with us. He wore his long Arab robe for the occasion. He drank coffee and ate cookies with us. We tried to get from him some of the history of his Fung people but he knew little. His knowledge of Arabic was limited. He left us to discuss our proposal with the two Moslem merchants across the hill. He returned later to say, "My people do not want you here."

We asked him if he had visited our Chali station. We wondered how much he knew about things that were going on in a thirty-mile radius. He had heard about Chali but did not know enough about events there to be impressed. We asked him if he wouldn't like to visit the Uduk people. We offered to take him in our car.

The visit to Chali was an eye-opener to him. Here were members of the Uduk tribe, in his mind much more primitive than his own Barun people, reading and writing. The Christians at Chali talked to him and told him about "the paper," medicine, school, and above all salvation.

We didn't press the chief for an answer until we were back at Maiak. "How did you like your visit to Chali?" we asked.

"The people there are very good," he replied. "They will go ahead of us."

"We would like to help you here, too," I commented

almost casually. I was feeling anything but casual. We were desperately anxious to open a station here to reach the Baruns with the Gospel before Islam swallowed them up. Much negotiation had brought us to this point. What the chief said in the next two minutes might give us our answer.

"Where would you like to build your house?" he asked without introduction.

"We would like to build here by the stream," I replied.

"It is all right. You may have it," he said and turned abruptly and walked away. Later when the district commissioner asked him about his decision, he said, "I have told them they may have the land."

When the chief left us, Joe and I sat down on our empty gasoline cans and offered thanks to God. The Lord had heard our prayers. We realized that getting the lease and building the houses might be much easier than getting the Gospel into the hearts of the Barun people. Unlike the Yabus, there would be some competition from Islam.

The stations at Yabus, Wadega, and Maiak would be the last to be opened by the Sudan Interior Mission in the Sudan. The Africa Inland Mission had been permitted to start a new work to the east of the Nile not far from the Uganda border. They would open six stations. This would be the extent of their work. We did not know it then but another era in the history of the Christian Church and missions was drawing to a close.

We should have realized that the tide was moving against us. Instead, we remained reasonably optimistic as missionaries often do in most unreasonable circumstances. As we began work at Yabus, Maiak, and Wadega, we did not realize that they would be the last stations we would open in the Sudan.

When Wadega station was being built, self-government was a fact and independence was not far off for the Sudanese. Local Northern merchants were amazed when, later on in the midst of the clamor for freedom and the end of colonialism, we made bricks, dug foundations, and started to build a second house on the station.

The Arabs gathered at the building site to discuss this Mission folly. "We are going to get rid of the British. We are going to have our own government. You will all have to leave. Why are you building a house?" The spokesman for the "Arabs" believed that independence would find part of its expression in the expulsion of missionaries.

We had always defended ourselves against the charge that we were representing or being paid by our own government or the British in Khartoum.

In the Sudan mosques were built with money supplied by the Religious Affairs Department. Moslem religious leaders were trained in government institutions. It was reasonable for these same Moslems to believe that we, too, were recipients of British and American government money.

Being actively Protestant, the idea of receiving support for our Christian work from any government was abhorrent to us. Our own government later gave the Sudanese millions of dollars for roads, education, and agriculture. We wanted and received none.

The increase in the work brought about by the opening of the Yabus, Maiak, and Wadega stations made the opening of a hospital in the area imperative. Friends of the late Dr. Robert C. McQuilkin, former president of Columbia Bible College in South Carolina, contributed most of the funds for the building of the McQuilkin Memorial Hospital. Doro was chosen as the site.

When the hospital was commissioned, nurses and doctors began to work on the huge backlog of ulcers with their scar tissue. T.B. patients were treated. Tumors were removed. Kala azar, cerebrospinal meningitis, and yellow fever brought high attendances at the hospital. Khartoum missionaries found it increasingly difficult to house the many workers who passed through the city or who needed to spend several weeks in the capital for business or medical reasons. There were sixty-eight missionaries on the roll and the number of children had passed thirty.

The Sudan government, still British in 1950, gave us a plot of ground in a new area of Khartoum on which to build our headquarters. We built a chapel, a hostel, and a small office block. By the time the building work was completed, we had begun to wonder whether, in the end, we or other people, unknown to us, would occupy our new headquarters.

16

✖✖✖✖✖✖✖✖✖✖✖✖✖✖✖✖✖✖✖

RAF and MAF

✖✖✖✖✖✖✖✖✖✖✖✖✖✖✖✖✖✖✖

As THE NUMBER of missionaries and children living on our stations grew, our concern for them in their isolation during the rainy season increased. The missionaries themselves had an unconscious anxiety. What happens when a child or adult becomes dangerously ill?

Even when the hospital at Doro was completed, it was almost impossible to get a person thirty miles through mud and rain to the doctor.

All our stations were affected by the runoff of rainwater from the Ethiopian highlands onto the flat Sudan plain. The water in our area did not head northward to join the Blue Nile; it seeped across one hundred and fifty miles of flat bush and grassland to the White Nile. Jeeps were famous for their ability to get through under any circumstances. But Jeeps were not invincible. And the authorities would not let cars be driven on the roads when they were wet lest they leave deep ruts which would harden to cement in the dry season.

So we had to look for something else. We dreamed of aircraft. But even our dreams seemed extravagant. Should missionaries travel in such ease? Would this kind of travel separate us farther from the people we were trying to reach by friendship and love?

We seldom thought of items of equipment only as means of easing the problems of living or travel. We thought of the implications. "How will this affect our relations with the people around us?" Somehow the needs of the people had to be related rightly to the needs of the missionaries.

The people were not given any help during the periods when missionaries had to spend twenty-four hours a day trying to keep one of their babies alive without medical aid of any kind. How could the anxiety which cut so deeply into efficiency be allayed?

Our missionaries were devoted to their work and to the Lord. They did not ask for aircraft nor did they seek escape from the anxieties brought on by isolation. They trusted the Lord and faced possible tragedy year after year. But relief was on the way.

When World War II ended, pilots and engineers left the Royal Air Force and the United States Air Force in large numbers. Some of them were dedicated Christians. They began to look for ways to use their aviation skills in the Lord's service. In America some of them got together and formed the Missionary Aviation Fellowship. A similar fellowship was formed in England.

The purpose of the founders of these organizations was to provide flying services for missionaries in isolated parts of the world.

When we discussed with British officials the use of

aircraft in our work, we received kindly smiles. We should have known what the officials knew: that the swamps and deserts of the Sudan would make the use of aircraft extremely dangerous. The authorities could expect frequent calls to go in search of missing missionary aircraft.

The authorities agreed to ask the Royal Air Force to make a survey of our stations and to report on the advisability of giving us permission to use a plane in our communications. This was early in 1946.

A plane of the Royal Air Force Squadron based in Khartoum was to fly over our stations on one of its routine flights. The pilot had been told that there were few roads in the area. He found traces of roads everywhere. None of them led to mission stations. He circled and zigzagged. There were no houses, no gardens, no buildings of any kind. There were no mission stations to be found.

The plane returned to Khartoum. The pilot made his report. It eventually reached the administration and we received our reply. "We cannot agree to your mission using an airplane in Upper Nile Province. The Royal Air Force could locate none of your stations."

We were never overwhelmed by the infallible findings of governments. There were a few times when missionaries were right and government spokesmen wrong. But we were in no position to acquire a plane and as yet we did not have a pilot-engineer.

In England former air force pilots and engineers were moving ahead with their plans. The newly organized Missionary Aviation Fellowship was ready to look for a mission field where its services were needed. The youthful organizers decided that Africa was in their backyard and should have their attention.

"We intend to make a survey of African countries," they wrote to us from London. "We will visit Khartoum on our way to the Congo and East Africa."

The survey was made. Information about mountain climbing was gathered the hard way in East Africa. The plane was caught in a down draft and the survey ended where the plane crash-landed.

Missionary Aviation Fellowship did not quit. Their main resource was gone, but they had seen enough to know where their future lay.

"We saw no country in Africa that needed our service as much as the Sudan," Stuart King wrote from London. "There are fairly good roads in the Congo and in East Africa. Missionaries in the Sudan are isolated for half the year. We would like to establish a base in the Sudan in order to serve all Protestant missions."

After the loss of its first plane in East Africa, Missionary Aviation Fellowship, which had become known as MAF, acquired a used De Havilland Rapide, a two-engine biplane made of plywood and fabric.

The Sudan government agreed to let MAF bring its plane into the country. If MAF pilots could prove that they could fly missionaries safely, they would be permitted to establish a flying service.

By this time we were corresponding regularly with Stuart King in London. He was one of the first ex-RAF members to join British MAF. He had earned his aircraft engineering licenses. Jack Hemmings was the pilot.

Hemmings let his plane down onto the runway at the Khartoum Civil Airport. This was the beginning of a new missionary chapter in the Sudan. Was this chapter toward the end of the book?

Before much serious flying could be done, Stuart, who was responsible for the MAF paper work, had to write up his proposals in detail for the director of civil aviation. The director wanted to know which airstrips were to be used, where new ones were to be located, and what plans MAF had for communicating with mission stations by radio.

Stuart arrived home one day as we were sitting down to lunch.

"I just handed in a long screed to the director," he said, a big load off his chest.

One of our American young women asked, "What's a screed, anyway?"

"Don't you know what a screed is?" Stuart asked "Haven't you ever heard of the Apostles' Screed?"

Stuart had been impressed by the lack of starting power in our Mission cars. Almost daily some trip to town was begun with all hands giving the car a push to start it.

"Now I know what S.I.M. means," Stuart said with satisfaction. "It means Seldom Instantly Mobile."

Aircraft were still keeping in touch with ground stations by wireless telegraphy. Every plane had to carry an operator who could use the telegraph key. Stuart knew the Morse code but the number of words he could produce per minute was well below the minimum requirement for a licensed aircraft telegraph operator.

He rigged up a key with batteries, hired an operator in the Department of Posts and Telegraphs to coach him, and settled down to long hours of drudgery. MAF's getting off the ground depended on Stuart's progress at the key.

All day long and into the evening the drone of dots and

dashes could be heard throughout the Mission house. Sometimes it faltered. Sometimes it was steady. Every evening Stuart was asked, "How is it coming?" Sometimes there were breakthroughs from the ten-word-a-minute level to the twelve. Then from twelve to fourteen. Then progress stopped and fourteen words a minute seemed to be the fastest speed Stuart would be able to attain. Then, after days of practice, the sixteen-word level was gained. It was a monotonous and endless task.

Stuart had other anxieties. Jack Hemmings did not have a commercial pilots' license, though he had been an RAF squadron leader. His eyesight was slightly substandard. The Sudan government would not let him do MAF flying on a private license. Jack returned to London. In the meantime South Africa had been heard from. Capt. Steve Stevens had been in the Air Force for ten years and had flown fighter planes during World War II. He had bombed and strafed Italian waterfront installations with a Beaufighter. How this high-tension fighter pilot would be able to retain his patience in our hundred-and-ten-mile-an-hour biplane was hard to predict.

But Steve was more interested in promoting the work of the Lord than in flying for flying's sake. He soon arrived in Khartoum to take over as MAF pilot.

As the May to October rainy season progressed in 1950, Stuart approached the minimum speed required for his license to serve as radio operator in the MAF plane.

Now the missions had to find the answer to a question. "When MAF was ready to fly, where would the pilot land the plane?" There were no airstrips ready at any of the stations. On-the-ground exploration had revealed that it would be difficult and expensive to remove trees and anthills and clump grass and it would take months to make a surface smooth enough for safe landings.

We had searched the area of our Doro station in vain for a possible site. Tall dom palms grew everywhere. If we were to remove any of the nut-bearing trees, we might lose the friendship of the people. Baobab trees, some of them twenty feet in diameter, squatted where airstrips might have been.

One day a letter arrived from the Doro missionaries. "We have found a good place for a strip just a hundred yards from our station," they wrote. "It will take quite a bit of money to clear the palm and baobab trees and huge termite hills from the strip."

A strip only a hundred yards from the station would be ideal. "Go ahead and clear the site," I telegraphed.

There was no labor market at Doro. Missionaries could hire a few men to chop wood and clear the grass from the station. During the rains these men were busy weeding their own crops. Money would not tempt them.

The missionaries decided that they would have to get the people excited enough about the coming of the plane to work on the airstrip.

They called the chiefs together. "One of those things that flies overhead is going to land here," he explained. "It needs a long clear place for sitting down."

It was hard to explain why the little speck on the horizon needed a long space in which to sit down. "It has wheels. It comes down fast and can't stop quickly," the missionaries explained. The Mabans had seen wheels on cars and trucks. They had cleared the roads of grass each year to allow vehicles to travel during the dry season. But the thing in the sky didn't need a road.

And besides when birds landed, they didn't need much room. They could land on the branch of a tree.

In spite of these arguments, the chiefs eventually decided that they wanted to see a plane land in their village. They had only vague ideas about its appearance. Trucks were useful and could be understood in a general way. Mabans hitched rides whenever they could. Trucks remained on the ground. What Maban would want to fly in a vehicle that had no support from beneath?

The conversation went back and forth.

"Where is the plane?"

"In Khartoum."

"What will it come here for?"

"To bring my wife and two children."

"Are you going to let your wife and babies go up in that thing?"

"It will bring my wife and babies just as soon as you make a place for it to sit down."

The Mabans were "talking it up" now. They had seen mysterious commercial aircraft flying overhead. They had never understood how the planes got up so high and stayed there. They had heard that men and women were in the planes. How small were these men and women? The planes that contained them were only specks in the sky. The Mabans well remembered the Italian air attack on Doro station during World War II. Bob and Claire Grieve, their doctor and his wife, had been killed by things dropped from aircraft. They had reason to believe that airplanes were basically evil. The two graves and a third, that of Mrs. Oglesby who died later, were right there.

The head chief spoke. "We'll clear the place," he said.

"We will pay all the men who work," the missionaries promised.

The word got around. If a place were fixed, an airplane would come down from the sky and the Mabans would be able to see it for themselves. Several hundred Mabans turned out to do the work.

It was not an easy job. The missionaries had a dozen shovels, picks, and hoes. Most of the work would have to be done with simple African hoes and axes. Anthills, built to a height of eight to ten feet by the unseen, silent termites, posed a huge excavating problem. The clay had been worked over and was held together by a termite adhesive. It did not break up easily. The Mabans dug at it day after day.

Mabans do not chop down baobab trees. Unlike other trees, they have no grain, no brittleness. They are pulpy. An ax entering the pulp remains there and has to be pulled out. The people brought dry wood from the surrounding forest. They piled it high around the baobab trees. They set fire to it. Slowly the pulp gave way. The trees sagged, sighed, and fell. In its fallen state a baobab covered more of the potential airstrip than it did when standing. The men hacked away at the fallen giants. They cut and burned. They carried away.

Others were cutting the grass from the surface and were filling holes. Doro had no stones to remove. Baobab trees, anthills, and brush finally disappeared. A smooth, sandy surface remained. It had taken the several hundred men eight weeks to clear the airstrip.

The rains were nearly over. The mother and two children had remained in Khartoum during the rains. They had returned from furlough after the rains had begun.

The missionary father had gone by mule the last one hundred and twenty-five miles to Doro. His family could not go with him on such a journey. Now as the airstrip neared completion, the missionaries were looking forward to a new kind of reunion—by plane. Though the rains were ending, it would be another month before the roads would be dry enough to use. Swamps dry out slowly.

※※※※※※※※※※※※※※※※※※※

17

First Flight

※※※※※※※※※※※※※※※※※※※

MAF HAD FLOWN several exploration flights in Africa. The first flight with passengers was about to take place.

"We have cleared eight hundred yards," the missionary in charge at Doro wrote. "It runs north and south in line with the prevailing winds."

Stuart King was able to tap out eighteen words a minute on his homemade telegraph key. He passed his test at the Department of Posts and Telegraphs. He had kept the plane in good shape in his spare time. I was waiting for a chance to get into the stations earlier than had been possible in previous years.

Finally the day of the first flight came. The Rapide was fully loaded with the passengers' goods and with car parts, lamp parts, and medicines urgently needed by our workers. Missionaries of all societies in Khartoum were on hand to "bless" this first passenger flight of the Missionary Aviation Fellowship plane. The first leg of the journey would take us four hundred miles to Malakal, Province Headquarters of Upper Nile Province.

Our prayers for the success of the flight and of the whole flying venture were ended. The missionary mother and her children climbed into the plane and I followed. Steve started the engines and gave his "all ready" sign to the airport officer.

The Rapide, despite its two engines, was not the liveliest of small aircraft. It rose slowly and laboriously from the long Khartoum runway. The flight southward was less eventful than our many trips by car and river steamer had been. The White Nile kept us on course.

Soon the Arab North gave way to the tribal South. There was no more desert. These were rainlands where grain could be grown without irrigation. Underneath and ahead, tall grass stood in and out of the water. Papyrus plants had floated downstream from the swamps and had stopped along the banks for a rest before setting sail again. Some of the papyrus "rafts" remained.

Arab robes and turbans gave way to tribal mixtures of Arab dress, shirts and shorts and, in the case of the women, skins. The Arabic language became diluted in this area. It was the *lingua franca* everywhere but the tribespeople below us spoke their own languages—Dinka, Shilluk, and to the east Maban and Uduk.

We flew near our Banjang station. We would have to have an airstrip there, someday. We flew over Melut and saw our station on the short stretch of the river that runs from east to west. It would be difficult to maintain an airstrip here in the cracking cotton soil.

Three hours had passed quickly and Malakal was just

ahead. There was a government airport there to accommodate the recently opened Sudan Airways services.

We touched down lightly and pulled up in front of the low airport buildings. The American Presbyterian missionaries were out in force. They were clearing airstrips on their stations and were getting ready for the plane, too.

We unloaded some of the freight and left the family in the care of the American missionaries. The adventure of landing where a plane had never been still lay ahead.

We were soon airborne again. Stuart and Steve had carefully marked their map. The Royal Air Force plane had not been able to find any of our stations. Could MAF do any better? We flew northward to keep to the west of the vast swamps before flying east toward Doro. This was the area between the White Nile and the Ethiopian escarpment which was inundated each rainy season by the waters that ran down the western Ethiopian slopes. On our maps it said, "vast swamp reported draining into the White Nile." We had followed the river southward to Malakal. Now we had to leave it behind.

We were due west of Doro. Steve banked and turned, following the course he had marked. Ahead there was bright green emptiness. The ground was featureless. There were no mountains, no rivers. There was much water but there was no shoreline. We knew we could turn back, if necessary, and come out at the Nile. But we did not intend to turn back. Stuart was tapping his telegraph key. He kept Khartoum informed of our exact position every half hour.

Gradually we recognized the western end of the Yabus

River. At least we assumed that this was what it was. None of us had seen the river from a plane before. We were getting nearer the Ethiopian hills and the swamps were more open. Now we could plainly see the snaky course of the river ahead.

"If we don't see Doro in two minutes, I'll start to make a square search," Steve shouted over the roar of the engines. A search was not necessary. Steve had Doro right in front of the plane's nose. We were shivering and sweating by turns. We weren't afraid. We were excited. This was the beginning of something wonderful, something big. And the signs were good. RAF had failed to find a single station. MAF had made its first try and had come in on the beam.

There was the airstrip, a big black scar in the midst of the undisturbed sea of green trees and grass. The strip was lined with the piles of grass and brush that had been removed from the surface. We flew over the crowd. There was a mass of upturned, black faces beneath us. In the midst a half dozen white faces turned toward us. No flight of air force fighters could equal the excitement and importance of this day.

The airstrip looked good, pilot Steve reported. He banked and came in for the landing. Our wheels touched down. We were at Doro!

The missionaries motioned to the crowd to keep clear. The Mabans would see nothing dangerous about the spinning propellers and we didn't want tragedy to mar the success of the flight.

We stepped from the plane into a mass of hundreds of happy Mabans. They might have been saying: "All the work of clearing the sitting-down place was worthwhile.

We have seen these people come down from the sky."
Some had remained safely under the eaves of their huts
until the plane was on the ground. Perhaps they remembered the wartime bombings.

Only a handful of the onlookers wore clothing. Almost
all the men carried spears, throwing sticks, bows and
arrows. Even among Africans these were symbols of
those at the end of the line. We had feared that the use
of aircraft might widen the gulf between us and the people. But as we chatted with them, there was no evidence
of this. Rather than thinking that we were displaying our
riches by means of the aircraft, it was more likely that the
flight was a confirmation of their suspicions that we lived
reckless lives.

We did not know then that some of those who were
standing by the plane that day in a few years would be
wearing clothes, carrying books instead of spears, and
would themselves ride in airplanes.

18

***

The Barrier

***

THE HELP the Missionary Aviation Fellowship gave us greatly increased our usefulness, especially in our medical work. When epidemics broke out, MAF quickly took our medical staff and supplies of drugs to the affected areas.

Kala azar, evil Sudan scourge, was slowly decimating the population of the tribal area from the White Nile Shilluk and Dinka to the tribes bordering Ethiopia one hundred and fifty miles away. This wasting parasitic disease, known only in parts of India, the Mediterranean, and the Sudan, had burned away slowly in villages for years. Periodically it flared into epidemics. Even in epidemic form it was not a spectacular disease. It slowly ground out its course until death took over.

In the Sudan sporadic attempts were made to discover the carriers of the disease. The dog and other animals were suspected. Until recently, a full-scale investigation had not been possible because of lack of funds and medical personnel.

In 1955 our nurses began to record an increasing number of kala azar cases. Sudanese doctors confirmed their diagnosis. Government health centers reported kala azar cases on the increase. The only effective drug was a preparation called Pentostam. However, if administered in slightly excessive amounts, this drug could hasten death instead of preventing it.

Our nurses became expert in recognizing and treating kala azar. The Government medical authorities, alarmed at the spread of the disease, provided free Pentostam to all our clinics. Once the Sudanese people realized that they were in the midst of an epidemic, they made their way or were carried to mission and government medical centers.

At our Abaiyat station, center of the epidemic, missionaries had to build additional huts for patients and their relatives. They dug graves in the cementlike cotton soil and then covered them with thorn brush to discourage prowling hyenas.

At last, after months of the care and treatment of patients, the missionaries saw the incidence of kala azar decline slowly. Our nurses kept on treating the many who had been infected. They and all their fellow missionaries had given themselves night and day to the care of the sick. In the midst of their devoted service to the Sudanese a letter came.

"The Ministry of Health is now able to take care of all kala azar patients. Your nurses will therefore refer all such cases to the nearest government medical center. No further issues of Pentostam will be made to your clinics."

Kala azar patients kept coming. They were turned

away. In some cases the nearest government clinic was twenty-five miles away, a long distance for a sick person to have to walk. Only those who were nearly dead would be carried to government clinics by their relatives.

Our nurses were not worrying about the loss of business. The medical work did not pay for itself. The charges for medicine were small.

The government action hurt because it meant "you may no longer show your concern for these people in this way." We were able and willing to help the sick people. But interference from outside made it impossible for love, compassion, and concern to be expressed. Nurse and patient were agreed. A third force entered making it impossible for the nurse to give and the patient to receive help.

On one of my visits to the Province headquarters up the Nile, I called on the Province medical officer, a Sudanese physician, to ask for permission to continue our treatment of kala azar patients. The decision which denied us the right to treat these patients had been hard to take.

When I entered the doctor's office, he stood to greet me. Then I sat down at his desk opposite him.

"I am grateful to you for coming to see me," he said. "Your nurses and missionaries were a big help to us during the kala azar epidemic."

"We were happy to work with you and your staff to get the disease under control," I replied.

"Now that the disease has returned to its normal incidence, we will be able to handle all cases ourselves. We will not be giving your nurses further supplies of Pentostam."

I knew it would be unwise to say, "There is still a lot of kala azar in our area." He was the medical officer and all information regarding diseases and epidemics came to him, not to me.

"I am happy that we were able to be of some service during the kala azar flare-up," I said. "We want to continue to help the people around us."

"We are glad to have the help of your missionaries as long as they keep out of our affairs," the doctor continued.

"We don't want to get involved in things that are none of our business," I said hopefully.

"Not all of your missionaries are minding their own business," he replied.

I did not know what was coming next but I realized that we had been walking close to the border of trouble merely because we were doing medical work.

"It was that letter," he said with increased warmth. "We had a letter from some chiefs asking us to allow your nurses to continue the treatment of kala azar patients. Your missionary didn't cover up his scheme very well. He wrote on a typewriter in English. None of the chiefs knows English and certainly none has a typewriter. I was supposed to think that the letter originated with the chiefs. I am not so easily fooled."

I was listening and at the same time wondering how I could convince this man that the letter did indeed originate with the chiefs.

"I don't mind your nurses doing medical work," he continued. "It is my patriotism that suffers. Why do these people go to you? Why do you represent them to us? They are our people. We are their government."

I knew the story. The chiefs were disappointed that they could no longer get kala azar treatment from us. Many of the people lived long distances from our Abaiyat clinic. Now they would have to travel even farther to the nearest government medical center. Their sick people would not be able to walk this extra distance.

The tribespeople were glad that our Abaiyat clinic was in the middle of their villages. Their sick had always been well cared for. They had confidence in our nurse and her helpers who knew their language. The medical work done by their government was less personal than ours. There wasn't the same compassion and concern as shown by missionaries.

This shouldn't have seemed strange to government officials and doctors. When medical work is a government department along with the departments of police, agriculture, administration, education, and veterinary services, it can't be as warm and personal as the medical work carried on by dedicated missionaries.

The chiefs had asked our missionary to write the letter for them in English. They gave their message line by line and the missionary translated it and typed it. In this offensive form it reached the desk of the Province medical officer with whom I was conversing. How could I convince him that our missionary had gotten himself into this trouble by trying to be helpful?

"I know about the case," I ventured. "The chiefs did approach our missionary and ask him to translate and type their message to you. He was wrong in agreeing to do this. I assure you that he did not originate the idea. It came from the chiefs."

"Of course the chiefs did not ask him to write the letter," he burst out. "It was your missionary's idea and he got the chiefs to add their thumbprints."

What could I say? We had faced nonconfidence on the part of various Africans all our lives. Officials, Moslems, even our friends were sure that we, like themselves, were not above "using influence" to gain our ends.

Sudanese like the doctor believed that our missionary salaries were paid, at least in part, by the American government. Even under the British administration the Sudan government subsidized the building of mosques and Koranic schools. There was no such thing as separation of church and state. The conclusion was obvious: all religious workers are subsidized by their governments.

We were never sure that the highest officials in government didn't think that we were actually agents of our own country. We did everything we could to get the truth across: that as independent missionaries we received no help from our government.

I wished such men as the doctor to whom I was speaking could have been with me in the office of our ambassador in Khartoum when we talked about missionaries being expelled from the Sudan. The ambassador had said more than once: "We can't very well intervene between you and the Sudan government unless you have been deprived of basic human rights." And I had said: "We don't want you to intervene. We have always told the people and officials of this country that we receive no help from our government. This is true and we hope that some day they will believe it."

I was sitting opposite the doctor still. In my discussion with him my color was against me, my religion was against me, my nationality was against me.

Being rejected and doubted was disappointing. But we did not quit. We had not gone to the Sudan to work only as long as we were understood and accepted. Our contract was with the Lord on behalf of needy Sudanese. No third party could break this contract apart from our being expelled from the country.

I knew the doctor to whom I was speaking. I knew him to be friendly, devoted to his people, hard-working and capable. He had been friendly to missionaries in the various southern provinces in which he had worked. They had always spoken well of him. But it was 1958.

A new factor had entered government-mission relationships. The doctor told everything when he said, "It is my patriotism that suffers." This was the new factor in the newly independent Sudan. We had surmounted many obstacles in our relationships with the Sudan government and we would overcome many more. But the doctor's little phrase bore testimony to a rising barrier that we could not easily overcome. We could not decrease his patriotism nor could we fit ourselves and our work into it.

It had happened before. In China the missionaries began to leave their work when it was plain that they were in the way. Our misfortune was that the tribespeople, and many Arabs, too, appreciated our help. Arab merchants and nomads and government officials often sought "our medicine." This popularity was working against us. My presence across the desk from the medical officer was just the beginning.

✳✳✳✳✳✳✳✳✳✳✳✳✳✳✳✳✳✳✳✳

19

"Your Work is Finished"

✳✳✳✳✳✳✳✳✳✳✳✳✳✳✳✳✳✳✳✳

THE TREND to limit our work had set in but there were temporary reversals. One morning radio telephones came to life on the stations as usual at seven. A feminine voice broke in, "Papa Romeo, this is Mike Kilo calling Papa Romeo." "Papa Romeo" was the American Presbyterian station at Pibor. "Papa" stood for the *P* and "Romeo" for the *R*. Our nurse was calling from Maiak. "Mike" was for the *M* and "Kilo" for the *K*.

The doctor at Pibor, two hundred miles away, was soon on the air. The nurse described the symptoms of some patients who had come in during the last two days. The doctor said he would check her description. At noon he was on the air again. "I think you should suspect yellow fever," he said. "You had better get a report through to the nearest government health center."

The nurse sent a "runner" to the telegraph office, twenty miles away. The next day a government doctor arrived. He confirmed the diagnosis. A yellow fever epidemic was in the making. Doctors in the tropics do not take this disease lightly.

Telegrams buzzed their way to Khartoum. Khartoum asked Missionary Aviation Fellowship to fly a pathologist into Maiak. Patriotism had to be forgotten for a while. A full-blown epidemic of yellow fever would be a blot on the good health record of the Sudan and would lead to quarantine measures being taken against the country by neighboring and European governments.

Sudan Airways pilots could fly to Athens, Rome, and London but they didn't know how to land doctors and drugs at Maiak. For Missionary Aviation Fellowship it was routine.

But Maiak was not the only place where medicines would be needed. Cases of yellow fever had been confirmed at Chali, Doro, and in the area north of Maiak where there were scattered government clinics.

MAF landed doctors at Maiak with large thermos bottles of yellow fever serum in ampoules. Little could be done for those who became ill from the disease. A massive inoculation of the uninfected populace was the only program that would help.

Police rounded up the people. Doctors supervised the work of medical assistants and mission nurses who gave inoculations by the thousands. Cases were reported from an ever-widening area. MAF kept flying in the drugs. The serum had to be kept refrigerated. Refrigerators on mission stations provided ice. Doctors came and went. They sent livers from dead victims of the fever to Khartoum for examination. The results were always the same, "yellow fever."

An American Navy doctor was brought into the fight

with a new device. He had a syringe that could force serum through the skin, thus making the slower process of injection by needle unnecessary.

Many of those who were exposed to the disease before they received the prophylaxis died. But it was not long before the death rate dropped and the epidemic was under control. Under the threat of a serious loss of life, the government medical services, the missionaries, and the Missionary Aviation Fellowship had gone all out to work together and to stop the progress of the plague.

Government medical personnel wrote letters of appreciation to the mission organizations and to the nurses and others who had worked so hard and so successfully.

At Chali, Nurse Martha Epp was commended by the government doctors for her work in the early days of the epidemic when speed was so necessary. She had gone to all the surrounding villages and in a short time most of the people of the area had been immunized.

When the epidemic was over, patriotism returned. "It is our duty to provide social services for all our people," government officials said. "We must provide government medical facilities for all."

Some of these "medical facilities" brought ours to a close.

Trucks rolled into Maiak, into Wadega, and into Chali. They brought lumber, hardware, and roofing iron. They remained and hauled sand and gravel from the dry river beds. Arab masons turned up to make and burn brick.

In each place the announcement was made, "We are going to build a clinic here." The government wanted to provide medical facilities for all its people. But more important than this was the closing of mission clinics which would result. These were taking care of the people in their areas. There were many places where there was no medical work but the government built its first clinics next to ours.

The missionaries were loyal. They did not complain nor did they undermine confidence in the government's medical work. When patients came begging for help, the missionaries urged them to go to the government clinics.

We still had our hospital at Doro. Nurses whose clinics had been closed could be used there. But this was not to be. Three nurses received letters from the Minister of the Interior ordering them to leave the country since "your work is finished."

Martha Epp closed her clinic at Chali and started on her way to Addis Ababa to take up new work with the Mission. She went to Khartoum to await the granting of her permit to enter the Kingdom to the east.

The Sudan was one of the favored nations of American aid. Money, goods, and advisers had poured into the country. There were new boulevards, schools, cars, trucks, and machines to show for it. There were also scholarships for study in America and free trips to the United States for government leaders.

"President Kennedy's personal plane will land in Khartoum to pick up President Abboud and his party for a trip to the United States. They will be guests of the American government during their visit," the newspapers reported.

Nurse Martha Epp was on the balcony of the airport building to see the formal farewell. Below her on the parking area was the gleaming Boeing 707, personal plane of the president.

Crowds had gathered to see the departure. An army band played. Soldiers stood at attention. Flash bulbs popped. Microphones picked up the ceremonies.

Martha watched as the president and his associates walked to the plane. The Minister of the Interior saluted, turned, and entered the American plane. He was the one who had signed her expulsion order. Before he returned, Martha would have left the country.

✕✕✕✕✕✕✕✕✕✕✕✕✕✕✕✕✕✕

20

The School Take-Over

✕✕✕✕✕✕✕✕✕✕✕✕✕✕✕✕✕✕

"ALL MISSION SCHOOLS are to be taken over by the Ministry of Education." The announcement was expected but when it came it hurt. The five Protestant missions affected by this order were the Church Missionary Society of the Anglican Church, the American Mission of the United Presbyterian Church in the U.S.A., the Sudan United Mission, the Africa Inland Mission, and the Sudan Interior Mission.

Various Roman Catholic orders had been operating schools in the Southern Sudan for more than fifty years. They had all entered the country during the British regime. The British had said that they could not find personnel to operate schools in the South. They would finance education if the missions would provide staff.

Mission education had become an important part of the life of the people in the Southern Sudan. Young men had graduated from elementary and intermediate schools and had become members of local village congregations.

Others had drifted from place to place, unsettled by their schooling but unable to make use of the training they had received. Many were "schoolboy Christians." Some became teachers, others medical assistants, clerks, minor officials, or were employed in business.

When the takeover was announced, there were about three hundred thousand "Christians" in the South out of a population of four million. Of these two hundred thousand were Roman Catholic converts and ninety thousand were Protestant. The number of born-again believers did not exceed thirty thousand. Most of the Protestants were in the area of the Anglican Church Missionary Society. The Roman Catholics had four hundred missionaries in the country. The five Protestant societies had about two hundred.

When the action was completed, the government had taken over fifty-one boys' elementary schools, three hundred and fifty village or "bush" schools, and six vernacular teacher training centers.

Many Southerners objected to this interference with what they considered to be their affairs. They had not been consulted. Some Southern teachers were glad to start working for the Ministry of Education. They were promised improved conditions of all kinds.

The actual takeover was arranged in Khartoum in May, 1957. Representatives of all missions operating schools were called to meet with officials of the Ministry of Education. The minister and the director made speeches indicating their good will and stating that it was the duty of the government to educate its own people. Missions were thanked for all they had done to lay educational foundations.

Though Protestant representatives realized that they had no rights in the matter, they did not want to give up their schools. They were training many children from Christian homes and so were conferring a double benefit on parents and children. But they did not fight back.

The Roman Catholic representatives had reluctantly agreed to the proposals of the government. Then the Ministry of Education received a communication from the Vatican objecting to the nationalizing of the schools and refusing to co-operate. This intervention from outside the Sudan disturbed the Sudanese. "The Catholics took our money for education without reference to Rome. Why do they have to refer to the Vatican to give it back?" they asked. The authorities went ahead with their program. They took over all the boys' schools. The missions continued to operate the schools for girls.

The Sudanese government was intent on using every means at its disposal to promote the unification of the Sudan. Northerners were sent south to teach Arabic in the schools and to introduce the children to Islamic ways. Where there were many Christians, the government had to go slow. In other areas, non-Christian tribal children were taken into schools and taught Arabic and the Koran immediately.

The Northern Sudanese looked upon the spread of Arabic as one of the major means of ending the division of the country. But the use of Arabic in the South would create new tensions.

Colloquial Arabic of a very low standard was the second language of the literate and of the laboring class of Southern Sudanese. Classical Arabic ranked far behind English as a third language. The Arabic being taught in government schools was not the fairly familiar colloquial form but the classical.

Like other Arabic-speaking countries the Sudan faced a dilemma that once confronted Europeans when their national language was the vernacular and Latin was the language of writing, religion, and speechmaking. At that time the Church fought for the preservation of Latin as the medium of communication in all learning. Only daring pioneer spirits in the fields of religion and education broke the hold of Latin.

The Arab countries have found no deliverers. Education in these lands rests on the learning of a second language—classical Arabic. This is one of the factors that has been responsible for the low rate of literacy in the Middle East. "Newspaper Arabic," a less complicated form of the classical, is now emerging as a useful vehicle of communication.

In the Southern Sudan only a few individuals have learned classical Arabic well. This creates the danger that a small number of Southerners who learn classical Arabic may become an educated elite, removed from their fellows and endangering the political balance by taking control into their hands.

The education authorities had always insisted that Sudanese school children be taught their own religion in government schools. The authorities agreed to continue the training of teachers of the Roman Catholic and Protestant faiths.

In new schools where there was no history of Christian teaching, it was difficult and eventually impossible for Christians to get their Bible lessons. Teachers of the Scriptures were not available or when available they were given so many other subjects to teach that there was no time for the teaching of the Scriptures. Pressure was put on the Christian children to take part in Moslem religious rites. Their parents protested to the headmasters. But it sometimes took a year for the parents to get satisfaction.

Many missionary teachers had originally entered the Sudan to do pastoral and evangelistic work. When the schools were nationalized, they happily returned to their pastoral duties. Their happiness was short-lived.

Letters began to arrive from the Ministry of the Interior. "We have taken over the schools. Your services are no longer required. You have two weeks to leave the country."

There were protests and explanations. "Teaching is not our principal work. We are working with the church." But the expulsion orders were irrevocable. Singly and in groups the missionaries left.

Some had done substitute teaching for a short time. Some had never taught. But even in their cases the orders were incontestible. The word "teacher" was the kiss of death.

✳✳✳✳✳✳✳✳✳✳✳✳✳✳✳✳✳✳

21

Good-by, Gordon!

✳✳✳✳✳✳✳✳✳✳✳✳✳✳✳✳✳✳

Wʜᴇɴ we had our evening worship on November 18, 1958, we prayed, as we always did, for the Sudan government and its parliament. We asked God to give wisdom, justice, and honesty to those in places of responsibility. When we awoke on the morning of the nineteenth, the government was gone, Parliament prorogued, and the Prime Minister detained. The Army had taken over.

A parliamentary form of government was well suited to the needs and temperament of the Sudanese people. It brought Southerner and Northerner together as no other administration had done.

During the parliamentary regime, the Sudanese economy was in trouble. The government, assured that Britain had acted selfishly in its purchase of cotton, decided to dispose of its crop elsewhere. The cotton did not sell. It piled up on the docks at Port Sudan. In addition, the crop was small.

The Sudanese began to realize that the British had not been cheating them after all. But it was too late. Britain had made her purchases of cotton elsewhere.

The government turned to the United States which had offered to give the Sudan both aid and loans. But the Sudan authorities were unable to act to accept the offers. The government was able to survive because it had the support of the leftist People's Democratic Party. But this party would not give its support to the acceptance of American aid.

In Parliament the parties argued and bargained while the country moved toward disaster. In the midst of the crisis the Army took over without opposition.

Tanks rolled through the streets in the usual predawn operation. The government radio broadcast orders to the citizens. "Keep calm, stay off the streets. The inept politicians have been dismissed. The Army will bring back integrity and prosperity."

General Ibrahim Abboud was the new president. He was surrounded by a cabinet of officers which was called the Supreme Council for Armed Forces. The day-to-day affairs of government were to be in the hands of a council of ministers.

Labor unions were banished. Newspapers became subject to censorship. The authorities claimed that thousands of telegrams were being received from citizens who were delighted with the fall of cumbersome, dishonest democracy and who were happy with the advent of strong government.

American aid was accepted. Relations with Egypt which had deteriorated because of the absence of a "Nile Waters Agreement," were improved.

The parliamentary government had to listen to public opinion. If it failed to satisfy the people, it could be defeated. The Army did not have to follow public opinion. It molded it.

Before its dissolution, Parliament had debated the subject of the disposal of the statues of Generals Gordon and Kitchener. There was agreement in principle. The statues must go. But disagreement on the method of disposal was so great that the two bronze generals continued to constitute the British presence in the Sudan for some time after colonialism had come to an end. When the Army took over, indecision was replaced by action.

"Gordon" was the most prominent name in Khartoum. His statue was set high on a plinth in the middle of Gordon Avenue near the palace gate. Gordon College provided the only higher education in the Sudan. The Anglican Cathedral had a Gordon Memorial Chapel. Perhaps the other memorials should be passed over quickly. They were the run-down Gordon Hotel, the Gordon Bar, the Gordon Music Hall, and the Gordon Cabaret.

Gordon, an eccentric, lived at the right time for heroes. The Victorians were always ready to elevate any public figure who clashed with evil or upheld the honor of the Empire in some far off place like Khartoum.

Gordon had been exposed to the Anglican Church from childhood but institutional Christianity did not appeal to him. When he met Christianity in the person of an army officer, he was captured.

Gordon had not found a new theology or religion. He had found that the old religion could be personal. He discovered that the church did not necessarily take him to God. He would have to find God himself through Jesus Christ.

In 1868 he wrote "My experiences showing the order in which God revealed Himself to me."*

1. Ever since I remember, I had a belief that Jesus was the Son of God, and used to have feelings of deep depression on account of my faults at that time.

2. I knew Jesus to be my Savior, and had assurance but was not established till I had gone through fourteen years of captivity commencing at the Crimean War till 1864.

3. At my father's death I was brought to think how vain the world was to give satisfaction, but after my brother-in-law's death, and consequent seclusion at Gosport for a month, God made me count the cost and concluded that His service should be ALL and that if EVERYTHING was given up, He would abundantly repay me in this world.

4. After a long dreary struggle (looked back on with horror) for eight or nine months of very earnest work God began to bring under my body in this way.

5. He gave me first to see that the fruits of the Spirit could be had only by abiding in Christ or being joined to Him but how joined was still a mystery.

General Gordon's unwillingness to become a member of a church cut him off from active participation in the communion service. Yet his meditations frequently brought him face to face with this memorial. He seemed always to hunger and thirst for God. He habitually arose early to read the Bible and to pray. He was fearful when

* Lord Elton: *Gordon of Khartoum.*

he thought that some of the necessary decisions were his and not God's.

Gordon drank brandy and smoked heavily in his early years. But he later confessed that these habits always seemed to him to be inconsistent with Christian living. He wrote, "The Sacrament is a weapon for warfare against the flesh and in particular for warfare against 'that immense serpent smoking and drinking.'"

Gordon was not a pietist. He was a practicing, not an institutional, Christian. He needed God in his thoughts, his plans, and his human relationships. His faith was childlike in relation to his friends and relatives. It was also childlike in relation to Egyptian officials in Cairo and British officials in the Foreign Office.

Gordon in China, Gordon in the Crimea, Gordon in England, and Gordon approaching death on the ramparts in Khartoum cannot be understood apart from his religious beliefs. If orthodoxy ultimately means to trust the death of Christ for salvation and to believe that Christ dwells within, then General Charles Gordon was wholly orthodox.

A general who looked over Gordon's shoulder, expecting to see sketches of his plans for administering Equatoria or relieving Khartoum, was surprised to learn that he was sketching one of the temples in Jerusalem. Topography, ancient landmarks and their significance for the present, always fascinated the general.

The topography of the Holy Land attracted him most. Others before him had suggested that the hill outside Jerusalem might have been the site of the crucifixion. Erosion had left the side of the hill looking like a skull. It was Gordon's endorsement of the site that gave it wide acceptance in the Protestant world.

Gordon was the first to claim that the "Garden Tomb" was the place of Jesus' burial. He often went there for meditation. None of the formal churches of the East had concerned themselves with this tomb. Hence it was unspoiled.

Three places closely identified with Gordon give the final clues to his character. "Chinese Gordon" was one of the greatest leaders of irregular troops in recorded history. Gordon of Khartoum went into danger unafraid because he believed in the providence and sovereignty of God. He died in the defense of Khartoum. "Gordon's Tomb" and "Gordon's Calvary" reveal the man who carried Christ with him into every situation. His faith in Christ was highly consistent with his success as a brilliant leader of armies. The unpredictable but successful General was the unpredictable but successful Christian.

By 1958, the Army government got around to the subject of Gordon and Kitchener again. The statues had to come down. The Army could decide later how to dispose of them.

Workmen appeared at Gordon's statue. With them rolled up a long-necked crane. Trucks brought pipes, cables, and tools. A hole was dug near the statue. The crane lifted a long gallowslike affair and set it in the hole. A rope on pulleys was lowered from the gallows and a conical tent attached to the end. The tent was raised and left hanging over General Gordon and his camel. Kitchener's statue received the same treatment.

The statues were not to be removed without ceremony. On the appointed day we were on hand to say farewell to Gordon and Kitchener. A Sudanese Army band took its place. The British Ambassador was there along with other dignitaries. The Sudanese Prime Minister was there. Around the official circle were hundreds of Sudanese and Europeans. This was an important if only symbolic occasion.

There was a ruffle of drums. Bugles added their martial notes. The honor guard stood at its stiffest attention. The band played the Sudanese national anthem. Then it played "God Save the Queen." As the band played, the tent was slowly lowered. Suddenly the Sudanese began to clap. Perhaps it is just as well that we will never know whether they cheered Gordon or cheered his removal.

Gordon and his camel were completely covered. Dignitaries and band moved off to repeat the performance for Kitchener.

Officially the statues were gone but the work of removal remained to be done. We drove to Gordon's statue once more. There was no ceremony now. Workmen were signaling the crane operator, men were chiseling away the last bits of concrete and steel that held the statue to the plinth. Finally the statue swung clear. It was lowered carefully onto a truck. The truck drove away. Gordon was gone. It was midnight. We went home.

Gordon College has become Khartoum University. But Gordon Memorial Sunday is still an annual event at the Anglican Cathedral. Gordon Cabaret carries on nightly. As for Gordon's statue, it stands on the cricket field of the Gordon Boys' School at Cobham, Surrey, England.

Gordon did not see many results from his labors. But he laid some good foundations for the Sudan that was to be. Slavery had to go. Inertia, bribery, corruption, and stagnation had to be eliminated. For sixty years the British governed the Sudan. When they left, the Sudan had the finest civil service in Africa and the Church was well established in the South. Gordon would have been pleased.

22

✳✳✳✳✳✳✳✳✳✳✳✳✳✳✳✳✳✳✳✳✳

The Moslem Sabbath

✳✳✳✳✳✳✳✳✳✳✳✳✳✳✳✳✳✳✳✳✳

IN MARCH 1960, suddenly and without warning Christians working in government offices in the South were told that Sunday as a Christian day of rest was to be no more. The Christians would join the Moslems in having Friday as the weekly day of rest. Everybody would work on Sunday. Christians were to have time off each Sunday morning for "prayers."

The equator does not cross the Sudan nor is there an international date line there. But somewhere near the tenth parallel there was an imaginary line north of which Friday had been the weekly day of rest and south of which Sunday was the day off.

The "day of rest" confusion began early in the century in Egypt when British authorities, trying to be broadminded, offered to work on Sunday and to make Friday their day off. Up until that time Moslems in the Middle East had not looked on Friday or any other day as a day of rest. According to the Koran they were to go to the mosque on Friday for special prayers.

Friday was not the same as Sunday. Most Moslems in government and business worked as usual on Friday except for an hour from 1:00 to 2:00 P.M. when they said their prayers at the mosque. Only a small proportion of Sudanese Moslems bothered to go to the mosques even on Friday. For Christians Sunday was not only the day for special prayers at church; it was the day of rest.

When the British took over the Sudan at the beginning of this century, they introduced the Friday holiday to the Northern Sudan.

In the South Sudan Christianity came to be the dominant religion. Since schools were operated by missionaries, Sunday was made the official day off for schools and government offices.

When the day of rest in the South was changed from Sunday to Friday the government had already taken over all boys' education. Missionaries were still operating some girls' schools. In the far south one of the women missionaries of the Church Missionary Society had been loaned to the government to serve as Inspector of Girls' Education. When she was told that the girls' schools would be expected to close on Fridays and remain open on Sundays, she asked, "Are you prepared to take over the schools?" This question may have had a great deal to do with what followed.

Our one girls' school was on Chali station. The Province education officer wrote that we would have to change the day of rest in the school from Sunday to Friday.

This change has been made by the government after a good deal of thought and consideration and the final decision has been arrived at because it is in the best

interest of the work throughout the country. It is therefore your duty to make this change in your school as
quietly and as smoothly as possible and it is also your
duty to see to it that Christians under your care are
given ample time for prayer on Sundays. You must remember that the Government's policy is that this change
of the weekly holiday should in no way interfere with
religious functions in which Christian citizens are required to take part on Sundays.

The school program on Sundays should therefore be
as follows:—1. Free time up to 10:00 A.M.; 2. Followed
by periods which should be confined to religious instruction, singing and art.

Thus the Ministry of Education, alarmed at the severe
reaction to its Sunday-Friday change, backed down but
did not recant. Purely secular subjects would not have
to be taught on Sunday in Mission girls' schools. Church
services would end at ten o'clock. The school girls would
study singing (in the form of hymns), art (religious), and
the Bible. Secularism would not invade our Chali Girls'
School on Sunday. The school need not work against
the church.

Still, the question of compromise arose in the minds of
many missionaries in all societies. Were we compromising
for the sake of hanging on to our few remaining schools?
Or could we accept the government's watered-down version of teaching on Sunday? It seemed clear that if we
surrendered the schools because of the Sunday issue, the
government would take over and the girls would soon be
studying the Koran on Sundays.

If we refused to accept the verdict of the authorities,
we would be saying, "We are not willing to teach religion,

religious art, and religious music on Sunday." We discussed the issue at length among ourselves and with the Sudanese Christians.

"You have to obey the laws or be sent home. You do what you must do. We will take care of our own relations with government," they said.

All the missions decided to accept the new weekly holiday in their girls' schools. By continuing to operate them, they would be able to contribute much to this part of the national church.

Meanwhile, the tribesmen in the far south were aroused by what they considered a new curtailment of their rights as Christians and as Southerners. They had not been consulted. The new regulation had been introduced without prior notice. But what could they do about it? They had no voice in the government of their own land.

The Southern Archdeaconry Council of the Episcopal Church had its regular meeting soon after the government announcement. The members believed that the government action was an infringement of their rights and liberties.

When they began their discussion, they invited the missionary members of the Council to abstain from participation. "This is our affair," they said. "We don't want you to be sent out of the country on this issue."

The Sudanese members of the Council discussed their loss of Sunday as a day of rest and then wrote a letter:

His Excellency,   Through The Governor
The President   Equatoria Province
The Supreme Council for the   Juba
   Armed Forces

Your Excellency:

The members of the Sudan Southern Archdeaconry Council of the Diocese of the Sudan, at their customary Annual Meeting here at Bishop Gwynne College, have been grieved to learn of the order which denies to Christians their Sunday rest.

The Council recognizes thankfully the peace and order which the Government gives to the people of the Sudan and respectfully asks that the order be reconsidered since it is a burden upon the conscience of a great number of loyal citizens.

> Yours faithfully,
> Secretary
> Sudan Southern Archdeaconry Council

The governor of the Province did not forward the letter to the president of the Republic of the Sudan.
He replied to the letter himself.

Secretary
Southern Sudan Archdeaconry Council

I am to inform you that your petition of 15th Feb. 1960, addressed to His Excellency, the President of the Supreme Council for the Armed Forces and the manner in which you have selected to put it, was a great disappointment. Worse enough, you have circulated it to eight offices before it had reached his Excellency the President.

The line of action you have taken in this affair by firstly discussing a Government decision already declared and openly criticizing it in a general meeting, and secondly petitioning His Excellency the President in the above said manner, is a sharp and unwarranted dereliction of the rules under which your Archdeaconry Council as a Missionary Institution preaching religion only is expected to confine itself.

I must bring it home to you and other churchmen, whether Sudanese or foreigners, that hostile actions of this nature amounting to such serious opposition and obstruction of Government policy which amounts to a criminal offence will not be tolerated and will not pass unquestioned. It is high time that you and your advisors should have exactly known the limits and scope of your religious activities and should have abided in it.

However, you have to be informed that the Government is taking a very serious view of this hostile attitude and your objectionable petition is therefore returned herewith.

The Christians knew what the limits of their activities were and they considered that their rights as Christian Sudanese were being taken away one by one. It had become illegal to discuss and to protest government actions.

Christians were not allowed to repair their mud-and-thatch church buildings nor to erect new ones without government permission. Applications for permission were placed with the authorities but replies were not received.

In the meantime the government financed the construction of Koranic schools and mosques in the non-Moslem South.

For the Christians their schools were gone and their clinics were gone. Now their day of rest was gone. Some missionaries were still with them.

23

The Last Farewell

MR. LUNN, Field Superintendent of the Sudan United Mission work in the Sudan, was on the airport tarmac below us with his wife. It was December 1962. The authorities had refused to renew the residence visas of the S.U.M. missionaries as they became due. In two years the entire staff of twenty-nine missionaries had been forced to leave the country. The Lunns were the last to go.

Their plane was about to depart for Geneina in the west. The Lunns would leave the plane there and find their personal and mission belongings stored in the town. They had been sent ahead by truck. They would take the goods with them and cross the border into the Republic of Chad. They hoped that some of their ex-Sudan missionaries would study French in Europe and return to start work again in the Chad.

This was the end for the missionaries but their work did not die with their departure. They left behind five hundred Christians in many congregations. In the last year before the missionaries' departure, over one hundred new converts were baptized. They left behind five ordained pastors and a council that would bind the churches and Christians together.

It was the year of jubilee, the fiftieth anniversary of the Sudan United Mission work in the Sudan. On the field it was the year of consummation. Government officials frequently told us that they did not distrust Protestants. They distrusted the Roman Catholics because they meddled in the affairs of the people and the government. Yet the Protestant Sudan United Mission was the first mission to have all its members expelled from the country.

During the fifty years of its work in the Sudan, the Sudan United Mission had established stations in eight places. The response to the preaching of the Gospel in the beginning years was not great. But by December 1963 the work was flourishing and had been turned over entirely to the Sudanese church members.

Among the first missionaries to reach the S.U.M. field were trained nurses. They opened clinics on most stations. Before long they were treating hundreds of leprosy patients.

By 1960 the nurses had two thousand such patients under their care. Five hundred were being cared for in a leprosy settlement. The sulfone drugs had revolutionized leprosy treatment. Each year many patients returned to their homes symptom free.

The S.U.M. missionaries studied the leprosy outlook and decided they could wipe out the disease in their territory in ten years. But it was not to be. As elsewhere in the Sudan the government opened its own clinics. The S.U.M. nurses were told to close theirs. The government continued to operate the leprosy settlement.

For some unknown reason the nurses were allowed to remain in the country. In 1954 members of the executive committee of the S.U.M. began new and serious discussions on the subject of translation work. The medical work was well staffed and results from the work were visible in the local churches.

Little headway was being made in the translation of the Bible into the five languages of the S.U.M. area. Some members of the committee believed that there was plenty of time in which to complete the translations of the New Testament. Others believed that time was running out.

Eventually it was agreed that if the work did come to an end, it would be tragic for the missionaries to have to leave behind them unfinished translations of the New Testament. Teams of translators were organized in each language area. Commentaries and linguistic helps were ordered from the home countries. Nurses and ministers went to work, aided by informants from the tribes.

By the time the expulsion of missionaries became serious, translations of the New Testament in the five languages had been sent to the British and Foreign Bible Society for publication. The nurses had a large part in this translation work.

While the New Testament was being translated, Christians were being trained to carry on the work of the church. A pastor worked with two missionaries in training a small group of leaders. By the time the two missionaries were given their orders to quit the country, four men were ready for ordination.

The authorities had said repeatedly: "It is our work to give our own people educational and medical help. You will be allowed to continue your purely religious work." We were also told: "We Sudanese have taken over the government of our land. Missionaries should train Sudanese Christians to take over the church."

When the two missionaries at the Bible School were told to leave the country, I raised the question of their expulsion to the Ministry of the Interior. "You said we should train leaders and turn the church over to them. Now you have made it impossible for the Sudan United Mission to carry out their training program."

The top man in the ministry called for the file. He read the correspondence between his department and the district officials. Then he said, "The local authorities consider it inadvisable to allow these two men to continue living in the area. We have agreed with them. We cannot reverse the decision."

There was no further court of appeal. The two missionaries packed their goods and headed eastward to Australia and New Zealand. But they were not through with missionary work. Before they left Khartoum, they were talking about their future work in West Africa.

We did not know how far the authorities would go in their dealings with sister missions. Living together under the cloud of expulsion drew members of all missions together. When we gave our help to the Sudan United Mission in Khartoum, we felt that we were helping ourselves and the Sudanese church.

Mr. Lunn, too, realized how close we were drawing to each other under adversity. We had much in common. The only thing that separated us was our memberships in different organizations. Mr. Lunn thought we should do something to remove this barrier that still existed between us. He wrote a letter to me dated August 5, 1960.

Dear Mal,

This is a private enquiry to find out your feelings before taking the matter further either with our Home Council or Field Staff.

Of late I have been wondering and praying as to whether our branch of the S.U.M. should amalgamate with yours under the general leadership of your headquarters in Khartoum so that you would have that added authority in dealing with the Government on our behalf.

For the sake of our home workers and supporters and of the S.U.M. as a whole it would be necessary, maybe, for us to retain our identity as far as the work here in the Nuba Mountains is concerned and the present method of financing it from Australia and New Zealand.

There would be a lot of detail to decide including the transfer of the Field Office and secretary to your office (if there is still one here!)

Well, there it is, and I have got it off my chest. If you and I can see the way first we may be able to help our field staffs and home organizations to do so.

Yours in Him always,
Will Lunn

Another letter which arrived from Mr. Lunn a few days later made it obvious that we had passed the point of no return. There would be no purpose in uniting our forces.

"Five of our missionaries have been told to leave the

country within fifteen days," he wrote. "This is the month of our heaviest rains and I do not know how they will get to the railway at El Obeid. They will try. If you feel led to mention this latest incident to our British Ambassador, go ahead. I do not know if it is the thing to do."

Nor did I know if it was the thing to do. For three days I tried to do my work but the action of the authorities in pushing women and children out into the rains and mud kept boiling up.

"We do not ask our governments to protect our work," I said to myself over and over. "Not by might nor by power but by my Spirit," I told myself. "The weapons of our warfare are not carnal but mighty to the pulling down of strongholds."

In taking the matter to the British Ambassador, would I be leaving the protection and help of the Lord? Would I be leaning on the arm of the flesh? Should I leave the trouble with the Lord and stop chafing?

On the other hand, if I failed to do something, would I be leaving fellow missionaries in the lurch? In appealing to the ambassador, I would not be asking him to protect our religious work. I would be merely saying, "The Sudan government is treating citizens of a friendly nation as though they were undesirable aliens." I would appeal on humanitarian, not on religious grounds.

If I failed to do something, would I regret my inaction the rest of my life? Would the Christians say, "Why didn't you do something to stop the expulsions?"

A hundred times I leaned forward at my desk and said silently, "Lord, what will you have me to do?" It may have seemed that there wasn't really much at stake. We had known times when we had to make decisions that

involved our safety. Neither our safety nor that of the
S.U.M. missionaries was involved now. But I felt no less
pressure to make the right decision.

As the first waves of anxiety and uncertainty subsided,
I knew that I would have to do something. I wrote to
the British Ambassador explaining what had happened to
the five S.U.M. missionaries. I did not ask him to take
any action.

I received a personal reply from the Ambassador asking
me to make an appointment to see him that week.

When I saw him he was sympathetic and anxious to
help. "It is my job to see that British subjects are not
forced into dangerous or uncomfortable situations," he
said. "It is not a matter of their being missionaries. I am
concerned about them as British subjects." The ambassador presented the case to the Minister of the Interior.
The minister asked questions about visas, residence permits and assignments that I could not answer.

I sent word to Mr. Lunn by Missionary Aviation Fellowship asking him to bring his files to Khartoum. MAF
landed with Mr. Lunn a few days later. Together we saw
the ambassador, who repeated what he had been told
by the Minister.

"One missionary claims to be a priest with two thousand converts. He is, in fact, a doctor claiming to treat
lepers. But there are no lepers there. This missionary told
the district commissioner and the deputy governor that
he really had nothing to do. The local chiefs reported
that they no longer wanted the missionaries in their area."

A wan smile wandered across Mr. Lunn's face. "One
shouldn't have to answer such statements," he said with
a sigh. "This missionary is one of the most diligent

workers we have," he continued. "He spends much of his time in the surrounding villages and the people ask him to return. He probably said he had about two thousand people in the area to whom he spoke. He does not claim to have many converts. Perhaps there are thirty. He has never done medical work. His wife had two hundred leprosy patients under her care.

"As for the statement that the chiefs have said they do not want the missionaries in their area," Mr. Lunn went on, "most of the chiefs have become Moslems. They do not represent the real desires of the people around them."

The ambassador thanked Mr. Lunn for the information he had given. "I will get in touch with the Minister again," he said. "I will tell him what you have told me. But don't count on any reversal of the expulsion orders."

We left the embassy. Two days later we were asked to return for further conversations.

"I gave the minister your version of your work," he said. "His reply was, 'Perhaps you are right. But in any case the five must go.'"

We were too accustomed to this kind of reply to be shaken. "I can only conclude that they intend to get rid of all of us," Mr. Lunn said, disappointment in his voice.

We rose to go. "It may be the intention of the government to get rid of all missionaries," the ambassador said.

"What will happen after you leave?" he asked Mr. Lunn. "Do you have churches out there? Will the Christians stand for their faith? Do they have any 'guts'?" The Ambassador chose the word carefully. There seemed to be no other way for him to say what he meant. He hesitated before he actually said it.

"I have no fear for the church," Mr. Lunn replied with vigor. "They are organized in local councils and they also have a council in which all the churches are represented. The Christians are strong, they have their elders and several pastors. They will stand."

Mr. Lunn stood before the ambassador. His work of a lifetime was coming to an end. His own ambassador could not help him. With the departure of the five missionaries, little of the work was left. The few remaining missionaries would find it difficult to carry on their work effectively. And how long would they be allowed to remain?

Yet at that moment Mr. Lunn did not look like a defeated mission leader. He was every inch a patriarch. Another patriarch had said, "Few and evil have been the days of the years of my pilgrimage."

Mr. Lunn's chief object had not been to build and preserve a missionary organization. It had been necessary to have missionaries for a few years to sow the seed and to build the church. The latter goal had been achieved. The work would not stop. It would continue in the hands of the Christians. They would stand.

We took our leave of the ambassador. We believed that he had done all he could to help us. It had not been easy for him. Showing concern for a religious organization is not popular.

Two years had passed since we had had our conversations with the British ambassador. Expulsion orders had finally reached all the S.U.M. missionaries and the Lunns down on the tarmac represented the end of their work.

Mr. Lunn had been faithful to the end. I had been enriched by his life. Why was he going and why was I allowed to stay? I remembered the verse, "We are no better than they."

※※※※※※※※※※※※※※※※※※※※※

24

The Act

※※※※※※※※※※※※※※※※※※※※※

MR. LUNN was gone. Before his departure he turned over to us his unfinished business. We did not think it wise to maintain much contact with the Nuba Christians.

On one station they were permitted to hold services in their church building. But at the other end of the station a Moslem religious leader was installed in the house recently vacated by the missionaries. A storeroom in the middle of the clearing was turned into a mosque. From one end of the compound the praises of God were sung by Christians. From the other end the Moslem call to prayer went forth.

If government officials thought they were on the way to solving the question of a Christian minority, Abri station gave them little cause for encouragement. Early each Sunday morning the call to prayer pierced the pre-dawn air. Some Moslems responded to the call. Few if any non-Moslems came to offer themselves as converts.

As the sun rose in the sky, Nuba Christians and seekers began to arrive for their Sunday morning worship. Dozens of them streamed past the mosque. The Moslem leader watched in silence. He had thought that the withdrawal of the missionaries would leave him with an easy task. The Nubas had been followers of the missionaries, he thought. Without them the church would collapse and the people would flock to embrace Islam.

The teacher could not know that those who walked past him had experienced a spiritual rebirth. They had not merely embraced a religion. They had become new creatures through faith in Christ.

If officials could not bring about the collapse of the church by establishing a mosque near it, they would have to dig at the roots. A pastor had taken over the operation of the Bible School. This was in line with numerous government pronouncements to missions, "Turn your affairs over to the Sudanese."

He intended to maintain good relations with the local and provincial authorities. He informed the district commissioner that he would soon begin a new term in his school.

The commissioner sent his reply by messenger. It said: "You have no Bible School. The school to which you refer was operated by the Sudan United Mission. If you wish to operate such a school, you will have to get a license from the authorities."

The pastor came to Khartoum to discuss this ban on his school with the authorities. "What does this mean?" he asked us. "The authorities said we should do the work in place of the Missions. Now when we want to do it, they say, 'You may not.' And what is this 'license' the D. C. talks about?"

The pastor had been in Khartoum two days when a call came from his district commissioner who had come to confer with his superiors in the Ministry of the Interior. I invited him to meet the pastor in my office.

When he came, the pastor asked him about the license.

"This is the license that is required under the 'Missionary Societies Act,' the official replied. Under this Act it will be necessary for all religious workers to secure a license from the government. This license will define the areas in which the applicant may work and will define the types of work he may do. It is no problem. If you apply for a license, it will be granted and you will be able to open your school!" We asked the D. C. why the Sudanese Christians were being discriminated against. "Moslems also must be licensed," he replied. "Ask the Moslems in your area. You will find that they are all licensed."

It sounded simple but it was not. In 1962 the government had let it be known quietly that "missionary societies" like the butcher, the taxi driver, and the shopkeeper would have to register with the authorities and secure licenses to cover their work.

The Legislative Supplement which contained the Act was a best seller. Missions soon bought out the printed edition and began duplicating their own copies.

While we did not know how we could conscienciously meet the demands of the Act, our greatest concern was for Sudanese Christians. Did the Act apply to them?

We referred the matter to our attorney. "It is very cleverly worded," he said. "Those who read the legislation superficially will assume that 'missionary' means 'foreign missionary.' But there is no reason why the legislation could not be used to control Sudanese religious activity also. This would seem to be its original intent."

The Act became the most studied piece of legislation with which we had ever been concerned. It was issued as "Supplement No. 1: General Legislation." But there was no legislature.

With the Army coup in November 1958, parliamentary government had come to an end. Since that time the legislating had been done by the Supreme Council for the Armed Forces. The only "legislation" the Sudan knew in the next six years was the work of these Army officers and their civilian collaborators.

The Army had taken over the government and in so doing had inherited the unsolved riddle of the Sudan, "How can the tribespeople of the South and the Arabs of the North be united in one coherent body?" The publication of the Missionary Societies Act was a serious attempt to answer the question. It was also an admission that religion was a major barrier between South and North.

We studied the Act. We discussed it among ourselves. Our interest was not academic. We and all pastors had six months in which to apply for licenses.

The Act began by defining what the Army government considered a missionary society to be "any body of persons, whether incorporate or not, whose sole or principal purpose is to convince by preaching any other person or persons to profess any recognized religion or any sect or belief related thereto, and includes where the context so requires, a member of any such society."

As we read and reread the "Act," we realized that the title was misleading. According to the new law, the purely Sudanese churches were "missionary societies."

The authorities would instruct Sudanese as to whom they could or could not witness. Speaking to a person about one's religion or witnessing to the Gospel was newly defined as a "missionary act."

While we were given six months in which to apply for a license we were to begin carrying on our work in accordance with the Act at once.

Representatives of the Protestant missions in the country met to exchange views on the Act and what to do about it. The tormenting question was: "Can we as Christians agree that we will not witness to a person of another religion? Can we agree to witness in certain geographical areas and promise to refrain from witnessing when we travel into another part of the country?"

We were concerned about agreeing to these demands for the Act was so worded that in applying for a license we would agree to police ourselves. We would agree in advance to keep the law. There was no other law in the land which required citizens to sign a statement saying they would keep the law and agreeing in advance to accept fines or imprisonment for breaking the law. Applying for a license was a matter of conscience.

The missionaries reported on reactions in their areas. "One of our missionary teachers has resigned to work for government. As a government teacher she will not have to sign an application under the Act. She will be free to witness to her pupils."

Another missionary announced that two of his workers had resigned rather than be included in an application for a license which would state their agreement not to witness to people of other faiths.

One of the Khartoum missionaries was getting more

and more agitated as he listened to the discussion. "I can never allow my name to be included in an application for a license. If I do I will be agreeing to refrain from witnessing to certain people. This is a denial of the Lord Who said 'Ye are my witnesses.' I will not so deny Him."

"What are the Christians out in the provinces saying about this?" a Khartoum missionary asked. "Have they seen it? Do they understand it?"

"In our area it is being discussed. Our church leaders can't believe that they will have to be licensed as a 'missionary society' to carry on their church work. They believe that if they as Sudanese have to conform to the 'Act' they will be subjected to unreasonable discrimination. They want to know why their churches have to be referred to as 'missionary societies.'" So one of the men from the provinces reported.

Another missionary had asked the Christians in his area for advice. "Shall we apply for licenses? Shall we agree to restrict our witness?"

"They said we should apply for licenses in order to remain in the country to help the church," he continued. "But they said they did not think they should apply for licenses. They believed that as Sudanese they had the right to carry on their work under existing laws."

We finally agreed that we could, as foreigners, accept the restrictions of the Act and apply for licenses in order to remain in the country to help the church through Bible teaching, the translation of the Scriptures and, in the North, in school work.

We also agreed that we would state in our applications that we were applying for licenses for ourselves as foreigners. Our applications would not cover any Sudanese Christians. We had "Sudanized" the churches. The

Christians would have to make their own decisions about the Act.

We agreed to have one of our number ask the Minister of the Interior if "it is clearly understood that we may explain our faith to anyone of another religion, sect, or belief who requests it on his own initiative."

Our meeting was not "organized" so we adjourned without making further decisions.

A few weeks later a reply to the letter came from the minister. "Explaining faith" is the type of approach which might well be a "missionary act" within the meaning of the law provided it is organized as the definition of 'missionary act' requires. If it is not 'organized' it is therefore not prohibited."

We agreed that the best way to keep within the new law was to keep our work as disorganized as possible.

December 1962 was approaching rapidly. In that month we would have to apply for our license in accordance with the Act. The Christian Sudanese were growing in their conviction that the law was discriminatory and that they would be disobeying God in agreeing not to witness to their own people who happened to be of another religion. "We cannot agree to neglect our duties as Christians," they said.

To us they said, "We need your help. Apply for licenses so that you can remain in the country."

We were coming to this conclusion ourselves. We would apply for a license. In so doing we would agree in advance to police ourselves. We would not wait to be detained for breaking the law in witnessing to a person of another faith. Other laws in force regulated the relationships of people to each other and to the government. The Act regulated the conscience.

25

The New Church

$\mathbf{W}$E SENT our application for a license under the Missionary Societies Act to the Minister of the Interior. We said, "We are asking for a license for ourselves as a foreign missionary society, not for any Sudanese associated with us."

This brought our relationships to the Sudanese church in our area into focus. If the church was to have its own separate identity, it would have to be formally severed from us by the formation of a fellowship of churches with its own constitution.

As a mission we had declared that there should be at least seven believers in a place before they could be called a church. Some of the churches in our area would not qualify. Others might just make it.

We had been at work in the Sudan for twenty-five years but in some places the results were small and uncertain. Only at Chali was there a flourishing congregation. Why did some of the tribes respond to the Gospel while others showed little interest? All were animists. All of them spent their lives trying to avoid offending evil spirits. Why did some find respite from their fears through faith in Christ while others would not even taste of this respite? It was a question that burned in our hearts by night and by day.

When the appearance of the Act made us take inventory of the churches, we realized that they were growing. Weak elders were showing signs of strength. Baptimsal services were being held. Recently illiterate men were reading.

To prepare Christian leaders for the churches, we had applied to the authorities for permission to open a Bible school.

"This is in line with your desire that the church be Sudanized," we wrote. The permission was never granted.

With no training center for the church leaders, we were confined to giving them instruction on each station.

When Christians from various tribes met together, they enjoyed fellowship which had not been possible to them as unbelievers. Faith in Christ broke down tribal fears and rivalries. It became normal for Christians from different tribes to seek fellowship with each other.

Organizing this fellowship was beyond them. Should we give them our Western type of organization and let them work it out as best they could? Should we prepare a constitution for them? Should we write out the rules of conduct and order? Should we list the officers? Need there be officers to keep the organization functioning?

Some of the church leaders had had experience with organization. The intermission and interchurch fellowship that met yearly in the South had officers, elections, and a constitution. It would not be entirely new to the leaders. Still, a fellowship of churches would have to be more closely knit than an interchurch organization.

We discussed our thoughts with the church leaders. "We do not know what the future holds for you and for us," we said. "You will need to stand together when the authorities ask you to apply for licenses under the Missionary Societies Act. Apart from this you need to be joined in some kind of fellowship to strengthen and encourage each other."

How would they get together for meetings and for conferences? Some of the churches were separated from each other by one hundred and fifty miles of deserted bush in the dry season and swamp in the rains. There was no public transportation. Sudanese merchants infrequently traveled through the area in trucks bringing trade goods and hauling out grain. They carried passengers on top of their already high loads. Travelers returning to their homes had to wait for the next uncertain truck. It would be hard for church leaders to schedule meetings under such conditions of travel. The church would have to carry on its work as best it could under the conditions that prevailed.

Across the continent in Nigeria the Sudan Interior Mission had labored for nearly seventy years. The Evangelical Church of West Africa had come into being as a result of these labors. Bible schools had produced nearly two hundred pastors. Elementary and secondary schools had created a literate church membership. Teacher-training colleges had turned out enough teachers to staff the dozens of elementary schools which had been handed over to the control of the church by the Mission. Some pastors had studied theology overseas. The church had its own missionary society operating in the unreached areas of Nigeria. The Mission operated secondary schools, teacher training centers, and Bible schools. It had a nurses' training course. It published mountains of literature at its Niger-Challenge Press. It broadcast the Gospel and Bible studies from a radio station (ELWA) in Monrovia, Liberia. It assisted the church and supplemented its work in many ways. But the church was on its own. No missionary could veto any of its actions.

In West Africa there was close co-operation between church and Mission. Having been given its freedom, the church did not despise its parent. It did not seek to revert to pagan practices. It maintained high standards.

Nearby in Ethiopia another church had come into being through the work of S.I.M. missionaries. During and following the Italian occupation the church had grown, spreading in every direction from the original centers in Walamo and Kambatta. During the occupation the church had worked out its own form of government and discipline. Its elders and officers were recognized by the people. Discipline was administered without partiality. The number of members was approaching the 160,000 mark. The churches in the various tribes had joined hands in an organization which they called The Fellowship of Ethiopian Evangelical Churches.

The name "Evangelical" was appealing. It had been chosen by the church in West Africa and in Ethiopia. The Christians in the Sudan could call themselves "The Evangelical Church in the Sudan."

It suggested faithfulness to God and acceptance of the Bible as His inerrant revelation. It was the true stream of life and interpretation that flowed from apostolic times to the present. It was the true spiritual "Apostolic Succession."

But the name had already been used for many years by the Presbyterians in the North to designate their church. We could not use the name.

The Anglicans had had no problem with a name for their church. It was the Episcopal Church in the Sudan. Likewise the Sudan United Mission had fallen naturally into calling their daughter The Nuba Church.

The Africa Inland Mission churches were now the Africa Inland Church. The Presbyterians in the Southern Sudan called their offspring, "The Church of Christ in the Upper Nile." The Catholics had no problem. Wherever they lived they were "Roman" Catholics.

As far as sources were concerned, we were deprived of everything but geography. Even geography failed to provide a suitable name. Some of the churches were in Upper Nile, some in Blue Nile Province. Some were on the White Nile. Most were between the Niles. The only name left was "The Church in the East Central Sudan." This name was adopted.

Before meeting with the Christians, a committee of missionaries drew up the first rough draft of a constitution. The committee was then enlarged to include national representatives from the seven churches. Before the first meeting was held, missionaries spent long hours explaining the proposed constitution to the church leaders. Tribal people had their own "constitutions," their own tribal sanctions, but nothing had ever been written or discussed.

The Christians would have to have a set of rules to guide them in the conduct of their church affairs. The country in which they lived had a government and a constitution. Every association of people had to have some kind of understanding that would help them to maintain good relationships within their organization. The churches in our area of the Sudan needed a written declaration describing its government and order. Once we had worked out the constitution and turned it over to the new church, it would be theirs to debate, to amend, or to follow afar off. As for us, we might be projecting ourselves into the far future of the church. The Christians would determine how long our influence should last.

Plans were made for an ordination service for Gideon Adwok and Harun Lual. Only a few years before, missionaries had watched Gideon as he worked for them and learned to read. He entered elementary school but he couldn't stay there long. He was nearly six feet tall and was out of place in first grade.

Our missionaries agreed that he was too valuable to the struggling church to be deprived of education. They sent him to Uganda. There he completed his elementary schooling in a short time and went on to study theology among the warm-hearted revival people. He returned to the Sudan just in time to represent his area on the first council of the Church in the East Central Sudan.

Gideon was a Shilluk. But he also spoke English and Dinka. His congregation at Melut was composed of Shilluks and Dinkas with an assortment of other tribespeople who worked in local government projects.

Harun was one of the few Christians from among the Upper Nile Dinka. He had become a Christian while attending the Mission school at Melut. He had completed his elementary education in Arabic in a government school. Then he had attended the Bible School operated by the Sudan United Mission in Arabic. He had just completed his work and was back in Dinka country.

The church in the area had only one ordained pastor, Paul. He had received all his training from the ladies on Chali station. I had conducted the ordination service for him, and laid my hands on him and had signed his ordination certificate. I had hoped that this would be the first and only such certificate I would sign. Once the church had ordained pastors, it would be their work to examine and ordain other trained Sudanese.

The Church in the East Central Sudan was a reality. Pastor Paul was the chairman of its Council. He, with the assistance of church elders, could ordain Gideon and Harun. He could sign the ordination certificates in the name of the Church. Missionaries could assist in the service.

The rains had begun and travel was difficult. I was on my last dry season visit to the stations. I planned to conclude the trip at the ordination service at Melut.

The Dinkas and Shilluks gathered in the mud-brick, grass-roofed church at dusk. Pastor Paul presided at the service. We sang hymns in Dinka and in Arabic. A missionary gave the charge to the candidates and I gave the charge to the church.

Then Gideon and Harun knelt before us and we prayed for them as they accepted responsibilities greater than any we had ever carried. Pastor Paul asked the two men to confirm their faith in Christ and in His Word. Then he pronounced them ordained to the ministry of the Gospel in the Church of the East Central Sudan. The Sudan Interior Mission was not mentioned.

I thought back a few years to the time of our arrival at Chali. I thought of the struggle we went through to get a few boys to learn to read. I thought of the few struggling Christians in each of the tribal areas. Our work had not been marked by mass conversions. We had seen the tribal people come to the Lord one by one.

What happened to the church in the future would depend a great deal on the competence and faithfulness of the three pastors. Our missionaries would continue to translate the Scriptures, teach the believers, and give their support to the local congregations.

There were no government officials in the area to join us in the ordination service. They were looking on from afar. They had said "We have taken over the government from the British. The church, too, should be Sudanized." What we had done that night at Melut complied with the wishes of government. The church in our area was Sudanized.

26

Last Days on the Nile

THE FORMING of the Church and the ordaining of the pastors was a climax for my wife Enid and for me. We had worked on unwritten languages, had done some translation work, had started some Sudanese on the road to literacy, had helped to rescue twins from certain death.

We had had a part in the opening of new stations and a hospital. We had introduced many new missionaries to their work. Through all this activity our objective had been the establishing of local autonomous churches. The Lord had permitted us, with our fellow missionaries, to see the fulfillment of our dreams.

We had seen mission schools taken over by the authorities. We had seen our clinics closed by government competition. We had seen missionaries expelled from the country. We had struggled with the Missionary Societies Act and the new relationships it imposed on us with the government.

It seemed that all that had taken place pointed to the ultimate end of missionary work in the Sudan. I had been the leader of our small band of missionaries in the Sudan for fifteen years, through all the changes independence had brought. I wanted to stay to the end if there was to be an end. But it was not to be. I would have to watch from afar.

We had said our farewells to many missionaries who knew they could not return. Now it was our turn. We said "good-by" to the believers we had watched as they grew. We said our farewells to our fellow workers and to the many Greek, Armenian, Egyptian, Syrian, British, and Sudanese friends we had made. We would soon be in America.

We carried with us the anxiety brought on by the Missionary Societies Act. It had been promulgated and announced. We had applied for licenses as required by the new law but no missionary society had yet received one. As far as foreign missionaries were concerned, they would not be needed.

The Army had taken over the government of the Sudan believing that it could do by direct action what the British and the Sudan parliament had not been able to do by negotiation. The officers made it appear that they had solved a number of outstanding problems: relations with Egypt, the economy of the country, the need for more schools. But the question of the divided country remained.

Unable to find a solution, they looked for somebody to take the blame. They returned to the old issue. The missionaries were continuing to alienate the Southerners from their Northern brothers. The missionaries must go.

"It is a source of profound satisfaction," the Minister of the Interior said as he announced the expulsion order. The Southerners were not consulted. The Northerners were not consulted. There was no parliament. The Supreme Council for Armed Forces acted on its own.

At Doro there were four residences for missionaries, classrooms where adults were taught to read, the hospital with its operating room, examining rooms, dispensary and wards and, half a mile away, a compound for fifty leprosy patients.

The translation of the whole New Testament into Maban was nearing completion. Leprosy patients were looking forward to the day when they could return home literate, redeemed and symptom free. Patients from a dozen tribes crowded into the hospital.

Dr. Lindsay McClenny and his nurses saw their patients for the last time. They could go to the government clinic two miles away or they could go home. The authorities said they would provide for the fifty lepers who lived nearby and who were under the care of the doctor. Most of the lepers went home.

The Christians heard the news of the expulsions but they did not understand it. The people who had done so much for them were leaving.

Dr. McClenny and his staff removed from the hospital their personal equipment. They put a padlock on the door. The station had been an active center for twenty-seven years. There was an accumulation of equipment, furniture, and personal effects only a small amount of which could be carried away. Most would have to be auctioned off under unfavorable conditions. The buyers knew that the sellers would have to accept the prices they offered.

The sorting and packing went on all day and far into the night. The Christians watched, still unconvinced that the sights they beheld were real. They watched as the small herd of cattle was sold. They watched as refrigerators were sold and hauled away. They saw the locally made chairs they had sat on so often loaded into trucks by Arab merchants and government officials and taken away. They themselves bought pans and dishes at greatly reduced prices.

The missionaries stopped in the midst of their hurry to talk to the Christians. It would have been easy for them to speak evil of the Northerners and the Military Government. But they had other things to say. "You may have hard times. Be faithful. Read the Bible. Talk to your people about the Lord. Gather for services on Sunday. Teach the people to read. Be loyal to your country and to your government as long as that is possible."

The last Sunday came. Missionaries and Maban Christians gathered in the church building. Its walls were made of mud brick. There was an open space between the walls and the roof, supported by poles. The thatch of the roof rested on poles and bamboos tied across each other with palm fronds. Swallows flew in and rested on the roof supports. Dust from the diggings of wood borers floated to the ground.

The people crowded into the building and sat down on the mud-brick benches. Would they hear some word of explanation? Would some reason be given for this strange exodus? The police were on the station daily to buy the missionaries' goods. They told the doctor to hurry. He must be ready to leave on the seventh day. No delay would be permitted. When the missionaries had gone, the police would still be there.

The leading elder stood and announced a hymn. The congregation joined in the singing. The Mabans sang sweetly, softly. They did not shout nor did they hurry.

A passage from the Bible was read by one of the elders. He did not have much to choose from. Although the missionaries had nearly completed the translation of the New Testament, only a few duplicated portions were available to the Mabans.

The offering was taken. How would it be used in the days to come? It was time to speak. The leading elder began. He had said only a few words when he choked with emotion. He sat down. Another stood to speak. He began. Then he sat down. Seldom had emotion robbed Mabans of the ability to speak. Never before had these men been so crushed.

Dr. McClenny stood to speak. "We do not want to leave you," he began, "but this is God's doing, not ours. The police cannot make us leave unless God wants us to go. He is the one who tells people what to do. He will be with you and He will care for you. Carry on the work of the church. Be faithful. God be with you."

In spite of the shortness of time, the missionaries did not use Sunday for their packing. They sat with the Christians answering questions, encouraging them, instructing them, having fellowship with them.

The last day dawned. There had been little sleep. Anxiety had added to the weariness of the departing missionaries. They loaded their suitcases, barrels, trunks, and boxes into their trucks. They tied up their bed rolls and packed the goods they had used during the last days.

The police were anxious. The last day was passing and the missionaries had not left. They stood by, rifles in hand, prodding, urging. The Mabans crowded around. Arabs stood in groups watching. Their feelings were mingled. Some were alive because Dr. McClenny had cared for them. Mothers had delivered safely because of the help they had received in the hospital. Would the government place a doctor there? If it did, could he possibly have the compassion Dr. McClenny had always shown?

At last the trucks were loaded. The missionaries looked on the crowd for the last time: friendly Mabans, some of whom had become Christians, Arab police, friendly, confused Arab traders. What would be the future of these three groups?

There was a final prayer. The engines of the trucks roared. A cloud of dust enveloped the cars in the twilight. At Doro all was quiet and empty.

At Chali the scene was the same. The church there was larger. Pastor Paul was there to carry on. He was supported by capable elders. The members of his congregation were literate. And they had something to read. The missionaries on the station, all of them women, had completed the translation of the entire New Testament into the Uduk language. They had sent the manuscript to the American Bible Society in New York.

Months had passed while the Translations Secretary and his assistants carefully studied each page. Finally the work was approved, printed, and shipped to the Sudan. Hundreds of copies reached Chali just before the expulsion order was given.

The missionaries had dozens of empty cans in which powdered milk for the orphans had arrived. They placed a copy of the book of church order, a New Testament, and a hymn book in each can. Each was given to an Uduk Christian. Soon the church literature was scattered throughout the tribe.

As at Doro there was sorting, selling, and packing to do. Tons of equipment had been installed because of the school and the orphanage. All was sold or given away. The Christians were given clothing and equipment they could use. The church was left with a folding organ.

Uduks came running from all parts of the tribe. "We just want to look at you before you go," they said. They had meant to come sooner. They had intended to become Christians. But they had been busy.

On the last day the police were on hand to see that there was no delay. They seemed to be embarrassed by the crowds.

The afternoon hours passed. It was difficult for the missionaries to gather together all the last bits of equipment and clothing. Finally they moved toward their trucks. They were surrounded by Christians and unbelievers. All wanted to shake hands for the last time. The police shouted. The crowd was delaying the departure.

Then the people began to sing. In the last year a little chorus had drifted into the Sudan almost unnoticed. It had been translated into Arabic and into several tribal languages. Perhaps the Lord had sent it for such a time. The Uduk Christians sang it with deep feeling:

> I have decided to follow Jesus,
> No turning back, no turning back.

The cross before me, the world behind me,
No turning back, no turning back.

The Uduk people had never been permitted to forget
the past. It was always with them in the person of the
Arab police, the Arab merchant, and the Arab government official. The British officials had been gone almost
ten years. Now the missionaries were leaving. Would
the past be reinstated?

"Get in your cars! You must go! You must go!" the
police shouted.

The crowd fell silent. Pastor Paul prayed. Tears fell
from the eyes of an unemotional people. The last word
was "Amen"—so be it. The missionaries climbed into
their trucks. The police pushed the people back. The
cars moved slowly through the waving crowd. Then
they were on the open road. As they increased their
speed, the singing faded. The last words the missionaries
heard were:

"No turning back, no turning back."

Epilogue

THE SUDAN missionaries had sent their children to our Bingham Academy in Addis Ababa. They had taken their vacations in the highlands of Ethiopia. They wanted to continue their missionary work near the Sudan. They decided to go to Ethiopia.

There was not time to get residence visas so they entered the country as visitors. When the missionaries asked the Ethiopian government to give them residence visas, the authorities said: "The Sudan government has asked us not to permit missionaries expelled from the Sudan to reside in our country. We wish to respect the wishes of our neighbor."

The missionaries had to move again. Some went to our work in Nigeria, some to Liberia. Some had already gone home. Our missionaries in Khartoum and Omdurman were permitted to stay. In the North they could not do much to harm North-South relations.

Dr. and Mrs. McClenny went to Aden hoping that

their permit to enter Ethiopia would be granted. Ethiopia needed doctors. A year later the permit was granted.

Mr. and Mrs. Will Lunn went from the Chad Republic to England and then home to Australia where Mr. Lunn died of cancer and weariness. Several of his young missionaries are at work in Chad and in Nigeria.

The Missionary Aviation Fellowship was permitted to remove its planes from the Sudan. Its flying program in Ethiopia and in East Africa is growing.

Sam Burns is executive secretary of our Mission in Great Britain. Chuck Guth lives in Toronto where he does the art work and layout for our publications.

With missionaries gone from the South, the government was able to begin its operations there unobserved. The expulsion of the missionaries had strengthened the resolve of the tribespeople to separate from the North. They concluded that the military government in Khartoum did not intend to give Southerners a voice in deciding the future of their part of the country.

Some Southerners demanded secession from the North. They would not discuss any other solution. Others thought they might have a chance of coming to an agreement with the North if they asked for federation. But the North was willing to consider neither proposal.

Army units had been scattered throughout the South ever since the military regime took over six years before. Now the soldiers began to challenge Southerners. They jailed those who showed any resistance. Southerners fled to the bush. Guns were brought out of hiding. The civil war was on. In the area our missionaries had evacuated there was no trouble until the Army sent a unit to Melut town. A gunpost was set up commanding the church building and the house of Pastor Gideon Adwok. The tribespeople were alarmed. Some fled to places where there was no army.

As pastor, Gideon was in touch with many of his tribespeople. The soldiers took note. They entered his house to search it. They found money. "This is to be used to help the rebels," they said. "It is the church money," Pastor Gideon replied.

Then the soldiers found a list of names. "These are the names of the rebels you are helping," they said. "They are the names of the church members," the pastor replied.

There was no hearing, no trial. Pastor Gideon and four of his church elders were shot. Their bodies were thrown into the Nile which flowed silently by.

The people in the former Presbyterian, Anglican and Africa Inland Mission areas suffered most. People who were literate, who wore clothing or who had held jobs with the government or with commercial firms were killed if they did not escape into the forests or across the border to Ethiopia or Uganda.

Doleib Hill station was burned down. Harassed Nuer and Anuak tribespeople escaped through the night to Ethiopia.

In the far south, the two Sudanese Assistant Bishops of the Episcopal church escaped to Uganda. Their theological college was destroyed by fire.

In the North, news of what was happening in the South caused anxiety and fear. Northern civilians were afraid the Army's program of attrition might backfire and cause serious trouble. The fear that the Army was not solving the impasse grew.

Northerners working in hospitals and schools in the

South had to close their institutions and return to the North. They brought with them tales of the brutality of their own Army. They told of savage Southern reaction.

The Northern Sudanese had long since tired of the inept rule of the generals. The Army had told them only what it had wanted them to know. It had extolled itself and its government in its publications. Sudanese enchantment with military efficiency and honesty was ending in disillusionment.

The Northerners did not love the Southerners. Neither did they love the Army's way of finding a solution by destroying the people of the South.

Resentment grew in the North. Moslems and Christians, Northerners and Southerners living in the North, had had enough.

They had nothing with which to fight the Army. So they resorted to nonviolent noncooperation. With one accord they left their jobs. The post office closed. Newspapers could not print. Government offices stood empty. The government radio station fell silent. Railway crews brought their trains into the stations and left them. Employees at the Khartoum airport left their radios and fuel stations. International flights had to overfly the city.

General Abboud trembled in his palace. He could not communicate with the people. His radio was dead. He had been aware of the rising tide of hatred toward the military regime. He was tired of his nonmilitary functions.

He called his Supreme Council for Armed Forces. They had had a free hand in running the country as they wished. They had failed. The generals voted to return to their barracks. The military regime collapsed.

General Abboud had to hand the reins of government to somebody. He called the man most likely to find a way to bridge the gulf between South and North.

Sirr el Khatim was not a politician. He was not a political administrator. He was an educator. He had spent most of his adult life in the South working with British administrators and missionaries. He had been an Inspector of Education. Since nearly all the schools in the South had been run by missions, most of his work had been with missionaries.

Southerners knew him well and respected him. When the British departed, he had been appointed to the top education post in the South. He became Assistant Director of Education for the Southern Provinces. When the government took over the mission schools, they became his responsibility.

We knew Sirr el Khatim well. We respected his ability and his integrity. The Southern people accepted and trusted him.

General Abboud called him to his office. He turned over the responsibilities of interim government to the educator and departed for England.

The strike quickly ended. There was rejoicing throughout the Sudan. The unpopular Army regime had been brought down by the unarmed will of the people.

Southerners and Northerners were sure their new prime minister would reunite the country. But reunion was the very thing the Southerners did not want. They wanted independence from the North. They might settle for federation. The North was willing to accept neither proposal from the Southerners. The country must be united.

Hope, which had flourished for so short a time, vanished. The Southern rebels resumed their harassment of Northern army units, police, and administrators. They controlled an area as large as Texas except for the towns.

The exodus of Southerners to the Congo, Uganda, Kenya, and Ethiopia slowed with the collapse of the Army regime. It soon got under way again. Exiles published their complaints exposing Army brutality. Military units, instead of withdrawing from the South, were giving new instructions by the new government.

The Southerners themselves were divided. The rebels in the bush and forest were determined to keep up their fight until independence was granted to the South or until death took over. Southerners in exile were willing to meet with the government in Khartoum to find a solution at the conference table. The divided South now faced a united North. Some Northerners had said, "Let the Southern people have the swamps and forest." Now they said, "To which Southerners shall we give the administration of the South?"

A "round table" discussion between Northern officials and Southern representatives came to nothing. In the South planes bombed hapless villagers.

Moslems, trying desperately to find a place for their religion and culture in the twentieth century, declared that there was freedom of religion in the countries they controlled. There was no racial discrimination in Islam. In the Sudan there was little to substantiate either of these claims.

By mid-1965 chaos in the South was complete. Medical help was available in the three provincial capitals only. Nine tenths of the people of Juba, the South's largest city, had fled. No schools were open. Roads were not safe. People who had lived along the roads had fled.

In the spring of 1965 elections were held in the North and parliament was re-established. The interim regime of Sirr el. Khatim handed over the reins of government to the newly elected officials. The South was not represented in parliament. It was not possible for elections to be held in the Southern provinces. Two Southern leaders were given cabinet posts. They had a voice. Yet it was not clear which Southerners they represented.

The colonial government was gone. The missionaries were gone. Still the Sudan was unable to solve its problems. The bitterness, the racial and religious intolerance of precolonial days were still in evidence.

African politicians who were willing to interfere in the affairs of other African countries were strangely silent about the Sudan. Some of them had similar situations of their own.

Around the world Christians were praying for their fellow believers in the Sudan. They prayed for peace, for good will on both sides in the struggle, for the end of bitterness. They did not wish to intervene. They wanted to see the Sudanese, North and South, find their own national solutions.

Where the church was permitted to survive, Christians had grown strong in the faith. They had not capitulated to the Northerners in order to survive. They were willing to die rather than turn their backs on the Lord.

Thousands of Southerners have been killed. Thousands have fled to exile in other African countries. Peace may return. Those who survive may return to their homeland. For them it will never be the same.

Our work came to an end. We left the Sudan knowing that our main objective—the establishment of the Church of Jesus Christ in our area—had been reached. That church was now a fact. Congregations were meeting at Banjang and Melut on the Nile. Others were worshiping at Yabus, Wadega, Doro, and Chali. A few believers were working together at Maiak.

The Christians in these places were not only meeting in their churches but their Christian living and witness was changing and improving life all around them. And Moslems were taking note.

BIBLIOGRAPHY

DUNCAN, J. S. R.: *The Sudan, a Record of Achievement.* London and Edinburgh, William Blackwood and Sons, 1952.
———: *The Sudan's Path to Independence.* London and Edinburgh, William Blackwood and Sons, 1957.
ELTON, LORD: *Gordon of Khartoum.* New York, Alfred A. Knopf, 1955.
HOLT, P. M.: *A Modern History of the Sudan.* London, Weidenfeld and Nicolson, 1961.
MACMICHAEL, SIR HAROLD: *The Sudan.* London, Earnest Benn, Ltd., 1954.
MOOREHEAD, ALAN: *The Blue Nile.* New York, Harper and Row, 1962.
———: *The White Nile.* New York, Harper and Brothers, 1960.
THEOBALD, A. B.: *The Mahdiya.* London, New York, and Toronto, Longmans, Green and Co., 1951.
Morning News, The: Daily newspaper printed in English in Khartoum.
Many stories from British and American newspapers and magazines.

DATE DUE			